Frida Kahlo

LOVE LETTERS

LOVE LETTERS

SUZANNE BARBEZAT

Introduction 6

LETTERS TO:

ALEJANDRO GÓMEZ ARIAS
A First Flame
10

DIEGO RIVERA
An All-Consuming Love
54

NICKOLAS MURAY
An Intense Romance
82

GEORGIA O'KEEFFE
A Profound Understanding
116

IGNACIO AGUIRRE
A Passionate Affair
122

JACQUELINE LAMBA
A Close Tie
132

JOSEP BARTOLÍ
A Visceral Connection
138

CARLOS PELLICER
A Deep Affection
150

Notes 156 · Bibliography 157
Acknowledgements 158 · Picture Credits 159

Frida Kahlo in San Francisco, 1939

Introduction

While conducting research for the book *Frida Kahlo at Home* (2016) in the archives of the Frida Kahlo Museum, I came across a letter Frida (1907–1954) wrote to Diego Rivera in August 1939, when they were divorced. He was in San Francisco working on a mural, and she was in Mexico, feeling despondent and alone. She described how the world had lost all its colour and nothing seemed to have meaning. As I read the letter, I was transported to that time, to Frida's sadness, her despair at being left and her doubts about whether anyone appreciated her art. Her pain felt real and present to me, and my heart ached along with hers, albeit some 75 years later. It was clear that, besides being a great painter capable of evoking strong responses with her art, she was also a gifted writer who could stir deep emotions with her words. She had the ability to draw others in, and, even now, we are still captivated and ever curious to learn more about her.

The basic facts of Frida's life are well known and often repeated: how contracting polio as a child led to her right leg remaining shorter and thinner than her left; the tram accident as a teenager that left her severely injured; her turbulent marriage to the muralist Diego Rivera, along with their divorce and re-marriage a year later; and her lifelong health issues that precipitated her untimely death at the age of 47. But her letters offer us a window into her thoughts and emotions, her character and the people she loved. Her voice comes through clearly, with her use of slang, her straight talk about people and things she did not like, and her uninhibited expressions of affection toward her lovers. We can peer into her mind and private life, witnessing her development from teen to woman. Seeing her tenderness, exuberance and her great capacity to love, we can appreciate her personality and get a taste of what it was like to be her confidante.

Frida lived and loved passionately. She had a few deep and lasting loves, among whom were her high-school sweetheart, Alejandro Gómez Arias, her husband, Diego Rivera, and her Hungarian-American lover, Nickolas Muray. The recipients of her letters were artists and intellectuals, and many were involved in politics. Most of them remained friends with Frida even after their love affairs ended, and many of them treasured her letters for their entire lives.

Frida approached her correspondence as she did almost everything: with creativity and zeal. From her distinctive personal style to her eclectic home decor, she infused every aspect of her life with her unique artistic vision. This passion and creativity also shine through in her letters, which she embellished with drawings and vibrant language, reflecting her artistic sensibilities.

As a teen, Frida wrote to Alejandro, her first boyfriend, during the times they were apart. These early letters show her spunky spirit and budding creativity. She had her own lexicon, which included invented words – one she used often is *buten*, which means 'a lot' or 'very much'. She would sometimes include words or phrases in other languages, mainly English or German. When her relationship with Alejandro came to an end, Diego entered the picture and would remain the centre of her world.

If at the start of her marriage Frida expected Diego to be faithful, she was soon disillusioned. He continued his promiscuous ways and was unapologetic. Frida looked elsewhere for love and passion and found it with a handful of men and a few women, while keeping Diego foremost in her heart. Diego had no issue with her involvement with other women, but did become jealous and angry if he learnt she was seeing another man, so she conducted her affairs in secret, often sending letters through intermediaries, meeting at different locations and signing her letters with pseudonyms. Many of her letters to Nickolas Muray are signed 'Xóchitl', and in letters to Josep Bartolí and Carlos Pellicer, she uses the name 'Mara', short for *maravillosa*.

Frida had other relationships that we know of, such as with Leon Trotsky and Isamu Noguchi, but no letters have come forth to give us more information about these liaisons. Her affairs with women are less well documented than those with men. We have the draft of a letter to Jacqueline Lamba in her diary, and a single letter to Georgia O'Keeffe in which she fondly remembers O'Keeffe's hands and eyes. Rumours of other affairs may remain part of the mythology of Frida's life. Did she have romances with performers Josephine Baker and Chavela Vargas, and actor Dolores del Río? We may never know.

Pages from Frida's letters are reproduced throughout this book. Omissions in the transcriptions are marked in italic by ellipses in square brackets, and editorial additions also appear in italic in square brackets. Frida wrote some letters in English, and the transcriptions, in most cases, preserve misspellings, inconsistencies in the spelling of names and unconventional or absent punctuation.

The correspondence collected here reveals the intensity of Frida's love, the complexity of her inner world and the enduring power of her artistic spirit. Through her letters, she invites readers into the rich tapestry of her psyche. Along with Frida's paintings, they leave behind a legacy of passion and boundless creativity.

LETTERS TO:

Alejandro Gómez Arias

A First Flame

You can't imagine with what pleasure I would give all my life just to kiss you.

Alejandro Gómez Arias, Oaxaca, c.1926

Alejandro Gómez Arias (c.1906–1990) was Frida's first beau. The pair met as teens in 1922 when they were studying at Mexico's National Preparatory School. They were both outspoken and outgoing members of the group of students known as Los Cachuchas, who were well read and erudite, but also rebellious and mischievous. Frida's first letter to Alejandro is formal and she comes across as a proper Catholic schoolgirl, offering him condolences on the loss of his father. Subsequent letters show her free spirit and growing affection and attachment to him.

On 17 September 1925, Alejandro was with Frida when a tram collided with their bus; she sustained injuries that changed the course of her life. Frida was bedridden for several months as she recovered, and again on other occasions as the doctors tried to treat her continued pain and health issues resulting from the accident. No longer able to attend school, Frida found that the letters she wrote to her friends, and particularly to Alejandro, were a lifeline.

In March 1927, Alejandro departed on a trip to Europe for several months. At the time, Frida was confined to bed wearing a special corset that prohibited movement. Feeling his absence more acutely in her confinement, she wrote to him faithfully and consistently. Soon after his return, he broke off their relationship. They reconnected in the mid-1930s, and she wrote to him a few more times, showing the enduring nature of her affection. Alejandro kept her letters to him, as well as her portrait that she gave him.

Known as a great orator, Alejandro was president of the National Confederation of Students and was deeply involved in the Mexican student movement of 1929. He went on to become a lawyer and professor of Mexican History and Literature, and a highly respected political journalist.

1922
15 December

Mexico, 15 December 1922

Alejandro:
I am so sorry for what happened to you and from my heart I truly offer you the most profound condolences.

The only thing I can advise as your friend is that you have enough strength of will to endure these difficulties that the Lord Our God sends us as a test of pain since we come to the world to suffer.

I have felt this grief in my soul and I ask God to give you enough grace and strength to bring you comfort.

Frieda

1923
10 August

Coyoacán, 10 August 1923

Alex: I received your letter at 7pm yesterday when I least expected anyone to remember me, least of all Don Alejandro, but fortunately I was mistaken. You don't know how pleased I was that you trusted me as a true friend and you spoke to me as you had never spoken to me before, because although you tell me with a bit of irony that I am so superior and I am so far beyond you, I understand the essence *[of what you say]* and not what others would understand… and you ask me to give you advice, something I would do with all my heart if my little experience of 15 years was worth anything, but if good intentions are enough for you, not only my humble advice is yours, but all of me.
Well Alex, write to me often and long, the longer the better, and meanwhile receive all the love from

Frieda
P.S. Say hello to Chong Lee and to your little sister from me.

México a 15 de Diciembre de 1922.

Alejandro:

He sentido muchísimo lo que te ha pasado y verdaderamente sale de mi corazón el pésame más grande.

Lo único que, como amiga te aconsejo es que tengas la bastante fuerza de voluntad para soportar semejantes penas que Dios Nuestro Señor nos manda como una prueba de dolor supuesto que al mundo venimos a sufrir.

He sentido en el alma esa pena y lo que le pido a Dios es que te de la gracia y la fuerza suficiente para conformarte.

Frieda.

1924
18 August

Monday 18 August 1924

Alex: This afternoon when you called I wasn't able to be at the dairy at exactly half past three, but they sent for me. When I got there the phone was hung up and I couldn't call you back – will you forgive me Alex? You see, it wasn't my fault.*[...]*

Hey, in ten days there's going to be a big dance at your friend Chelo's house and it's going to be a costume party, so I have to go get an outfit ahead of time and that's going to be the excuse to go on an outing with the owner of Panchito Pimentel,[1] right?

If I can't see you in the next few days, come to the village *[Coyoacán]* on Wednesday. Call me by phone at half past three, I'll be sure to be there, ok? But first, answer this little letter as soon as you can.*[...]*

Now I'm going to read Salambo until half past 10, it's 8 o'clock now, and then the Bible in three volumes and, finally, think for a while about huge scientific problems and then go to bed, and sleep until half past 7 in the morning, eh? Until tomorrow, may we have a good night and may we both think that great friends must love each other very, very much, much, much, much, much, mucho... with 'm' for music or for 'mundo'.

> First premise – Great friends must love each other a lot.
> Second premise – Alex and Friducha are great friends.
> Conclusion – Therefore, Alex and Friducha must love each other a lot.
> Grade 4. M. Cevallos

A little kiss without Pancho Pimentel getting too excited, eh?
A girl who loves you more than ever.
Frieda

[Drawing of her head on a pedestal.]
Statue of your pal. I barely escaped being born beheaded because of my very small snout.

[Drawing of a heart pierced by an arrow.]
I love you very much, etc.... kisses.

1924
14 September

Don't tear her because she is very pretty.
One ideal type.

14 September 1924. Sunday night.

My Alex, since I won't see you for two days and I miss you so much, I'm writing you this so that you will start to believe something that you don't believe, but which is very true.

Who knows when this letter will reach you, because I don't know if there will be any post tomorrow, but in any case I think *[this letter]* will do for what I told you before.

From the little doll above, you can see what progress I've made with my drawing, can't you? Now you know that I'm a prodigy in matters of art! So be careful not to find fault with this admirable psychological and artistic study of one 'payment' (one ideal type).

Hey, my kindred spirit, don't forget to call me on Tuesday at half past three, alright? I've been thinking about you these past few days and I hope there is a boy who has done the same, who I think is Panchito Pimentel's owner... that is, not the same one. You know what I mean... think of Mi... guel de Iturbide.

ALEJANDRO GÓMEZ ARIAS

¡No la vayas a romper porque está muy bonita!

Une tipo ideal.

14 de Septiembre de 1924. Domingo en la noche.

Mi Alex: Como te voy a dejar de ver dos días y te extraño mucho te escribo ésta para que vayas creyendo una cosa que tú no crees pero que es muy cierta.

Esta carta te llegará quién sabe cuando, porque no sé si habrá correo mañana, pero de todos modos creo que servirá para lo que te dije antes.

Por la muñequita de arriba, podrás ver, que progreso en el dibujo ¿verdad? Ya sabe Ud. que yo soy un "portento" en materias de arte! así es que mucho cuidado con ponerle peros a ese admirable estudio psicológico y artístico de ore pagchecha (une tipo ideal).

Oiga Ud. amigo del espíritu, no se le vaya a olvidar hallar el martes a las 3½ h°. Yo he pensado estos días en Ud. y espero que haya hecho lo mismo un muchacho, que creo que es dueño de Panchito Pimentel......... es decir no lo mismo. Ud. me entiende. pensar en mí....... qué de Iturbide.

Bueno me dispensas de que no te escriba más largo pero empezé a las 9 a hacer la muñequita y me tardé ¾ de hora astronómica y ½ de hora en escribir, como quien dice son las 10 y ya ves que a mí me da sueñito como a las gallinas, pero sigo escribiendo la carta en sueños y ya sabes al fin lo que te escribiría lo menos en mil hojas.

Que te quiere mucho — tu chamaquita linda (can de changa.
Frieda.

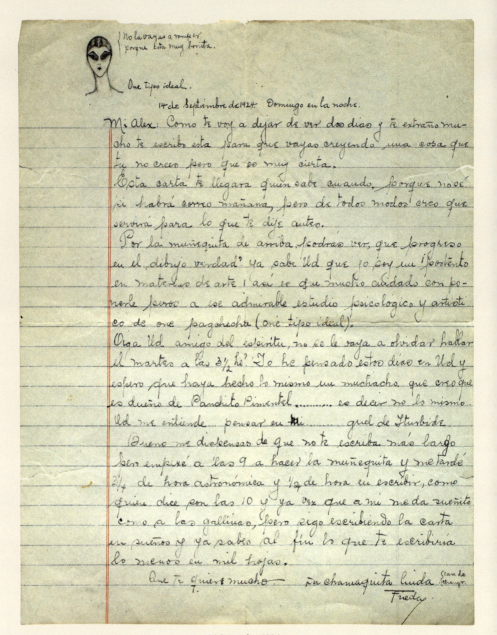

(Well please forgive me for not writing any more but I started to draw the doll at 9 and it took me an astronomical three quarters of an hour to draw and another half hour to write, so it's about 10 now and you know that makes me sleepy like the hens, but I'll keep writing this letter in my dreams and you know that I would write enough to fill at least a thousand pages.

I love you very much.
Your pretty girl (monkey face)
Frieda

1924
20 September

[Drawing of a cat with the words written next to it:] Another ideal type

20 September 1924

My Alex,

As I see that you don't want to write to me, let's see if by any chance you'll feel like answering this letter that I am sending you on 20th of September.

This morning when I went to see you, you looked very serious, but since I couldn't say anything in front of Reyna, now that I'm writing to you I want to ask why you were so serious with me. Maybe it's just my own worries or something really did happen.

Hey Alex, if this letter reaches you on Monday in the morning, I might be able to go and see you at the library. If I don't go it's because I had to go to Tlalpan, and in that case I'll see you for sure on Tuesday at the Ibero or wherever else you tell me that is not a bother to you, because I am very anxious to be with you, but who knows if it bores you to talk with your girlfriend who cares for you a lot but is a bit awkward.

Today I heard a ringing in my ears twice, and I asked for a number and they told me 7. I hope it was you who was thinking of Mi… guel de I.

Your Friducha linda 'one kiss'
Write to me please.

[Bottom left of the page in a rectangle:] Excuse the paper.

1924
25 December

Thursday 25 December 1924

My Alex: I loved you since I first saw you. What do you say to that? Since we probably won't see each other for several days, I'm going to beg you not to forget your little woman, eh?

Sometimes at night I'm very scared and I wish you were with me so I would stop being so frightened, and you could tell me that you care about me the same as before, the same as the other December, even if I'm an 'easy thing', right Alex?

You must like easy things… I would like to be even easier, a tiny little thing that you could just carry in your pocket always, always.… Alex, write to me often and even if it's not true, tell me that you care for me a lot and that you can't live without me…

Your girl, buddy, woman or whatever you like
Frieda

On Saturday I'll bring your sweater, your books and a lot of violets because we have so many here at home.…

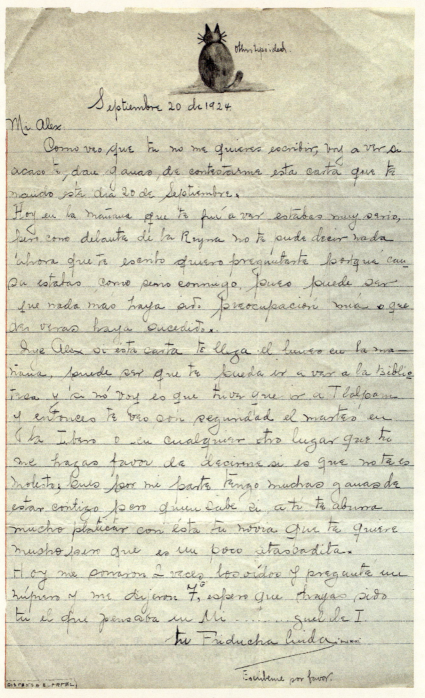

Septiembre 20 de 1924.

Mi Alex:

Como veo que tu no me quieres escribir, voy a ver si acaso te dan ganas de contestarme esta carta que te mando este día 20 de Septiembre.

Hoy en la mañana que te fuí a ver estabas muy serio, pero como delante de la Reyna no te pude decir nada ahora que te escribo quiero preguntarte porqué causa estabas como serio conmigo, pues puede ser que nada mas haya sido preocupación mía o que de veras haya sucedido.

Oye Alex si esta carta te llega el lunes en la mañana, puede ser que te pueda ir a ver a la Biblioteca y si no voy es que tuve que ir a Tlalpam y entonces te veo con seguridad el martes en la Ibero o en cualquier otro lugar que tu me hagas favor de decirme si es que no te es molesto; pues por mi parte tengo muchas ganas de estar contigo pero quién sabe si a ti te aburra mucho platicar con ésta tu novia que te quiere mucho, pero que es un poco atascadita.

Hoy me zumbaron 2 veces los oídos y pregunté un número y me dijeron 7º, espero que hayas sido tu el que pensaba en Mí .... guel de I
tu Friducha linda i menini

Escríbeme por favor.

20 September 1924

My Alex:
I loved you since
I first saw you.

What do you
say to that?

1925
1 January

Answer me, answer me, answer me, answer me, answer me, answer me

" " " " " "
" " " " " "

Have you heard the news? There are no more 'pelonas'[2]

[Drawing of a woman's head with shoulder-length curly hair.]

1 January 1925

My Alex: I got your letter this morning at eleven o'clock, but I didn't answer you right away because as you will understand you can't do anything when you are surrounded by people; but now that it's 10 o'clock at night and I'm alone with my soul, it's the best time to tell you what I think.*[...]*

Concerning what you say about Anita Reyna, naturally I wouldn't be angry in the least, firstly because you're only telling the truth, that she is and always will be very pretty and very lovely, and secondly because I love everyone you love or have loved (!) for the very simple reason that you love them. Nevertheless, I didn't much like that part about the caresses, because even though I understand that she is very lovely, I feel something like… well, how can I put it? Like envy, you know? But that's only natural. Whenever you feel like caressing her, even if it's just a memory, caress me instead and just pretend it's her, ok? My Alex? You'll say I'm very presumptuous, but there's no other way to console me. I know that even if there's a very lovely Anita Reyna, there's another no less lovely Frida Kahlo, since Alejandro Gómez Arias likes her according to him and her. Anyway Alex, I loved the fact that you were so frank with me and told me you thought she looked nice and that she looked at you with the same hate as ever; it shows you've been swept away and that you remember with affection those who you imagine have not loved you… something that is sure to happen to me who has loved you more than I have ever loved anyone, but since you're a really good buddy to me you're going to love me even if you know I love you a lot, right Alex?

Listen little brother, now in 1925 we're going to love each other a lot, right? † Sorry about constantly repeating the word 'love' five times in a row, but it's just that I'm very silly. Hey, don't you think we should start properly arranging our trip to the United States? I want you to tell me what you think of our going in December of this year. There's plenty of time to arrange everything, don't you think? Tell me all the pros and cons you find and whether you really can go; because, look Alex, it would be good for us to do something in life, don't you think? How can we just stay here in Mexico all our lives like a couple of dopes; and there's nothing lovelier than travelling for me, it really makes me suffer to think I don't have enough willpower to do what I'm telling you. You'll say you don't need just willpower, but first of all money-power or cash, but that can be got by working for a year and then the rest is easier, right? But since, to tell you the truth, I don't know much about these things, it would be best if you told me what advantages and disadvantages there are and if the gringos are really so awful. Because you have to realize that in all that I'm writing you, from the little cross to this line, there are a lot of castles in the sky and it would be best if you disabuse me once and for all in order to see beyond good and evil. (Because I'm still a bit of a dunce, believe me).

At 12 o'clock midnight I thought of you my Alex, and you? I think you thought of me too because my left ear was ringing. Well, since you know 'a New Year, a new start', your little woman's not going to be 7 pesos per kilo peladilla[3] this year, but the best and sweetest that has been known to exist till now so you can eat her up with nothing but kisses.

Your girl Friduchita who adores you.
Answer me and send me a kiss.
(Happy New Year to your mother and sister)

[At the top of the 2nd page:] Answer me and send me uno little kiss

Contestame, contestame, contestame, contestame, contestame, Contestame,
" " " " " " "
" " " " " "
" " " " "
¿Sabes la noticia?   1º de Enero de 1925.

Mi Alex: Hoy a las 11 recoji tu carta, pero no te contesté ahora mismo
porque, como tú comprenderás, no se puede escribir ni hacer
nada cuando está uno rodeado de manada, pero ahorita que
son las 10 de la noche, que me encuentro sola y mi alma es
el momento más apropiado para contarte lo que pienso (aunque no tengo en la mano izquierda línea de la cabeza) S. Mallén.
Acerca de lo que me dices de Anita Reyna, naturalmente ni
de chiste me enojaría, en primer lugar, porque no dices más
que la verdad, que es y será siempre muy guapa y muy chula
y en segundo lugar, que yo quiero a todas las gentes que
tú quieres o has querido(!) por la sencillísima razón de que
tú las quieres, sin embargo eso de las caricias no me gus-
tó mucho porque a pesar de que comprendo que es muy
cierto que es chulísima, siento algo así... vaya, como te diré
como envidia ¿sabes? pero eso es natural. El día que quieras
acariciarla aunque sea como recuerdo, me acaricias a mí y te ha-
ces las ilusiones de que es ella ¿eh Mi Alex? Dirás que soy muy
pretenciosa, pero es que no hay otro remedio para consolarme,
ya que, aunque haya una Anita Reyna muy chula, hay otra
Frida Kahlo no menos chula supuesto que le gusta a Alejandro
Gómez Arias según él y ella. Por lo demás Alex, me encantó
que fueras tan sincero conmigo y que me dijeras que la habrías
visto muy linda y que ella te había visto con su odio de
siempre, se conoce que eres un poquito llevado de por mal

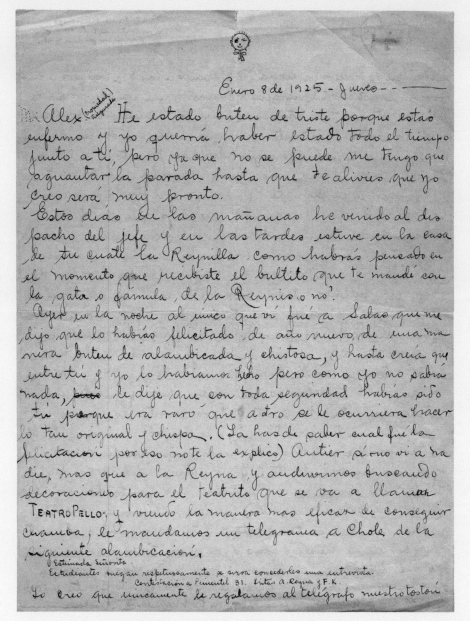

Enero 8 de 1925 — Jueves —

Mi Alex (¡notabilidad! Campoamor) He estado buten de triste porque estás enfermo y yo quisiera haber estado todo el tiempo junto a ti, pero ya que no se puede me tengo que aguantar la parada hasta que te alivies que yo creo será muy pronto.

Estos días de las mañanas he venido al despacho del jefe y en las tardes estuve en la casa de tu cuate la Reynilla como habrás pensado en el momento que recibiste el bultito que te mandé con la gata o fámula, de la Reyna ¿o no?

Ayer en la noche al único que vi fué a Salas que me dijo que lo habías felicitado de año nuevo, de una manera buten de alambicada y chistosa, y hasta creía que entre tú y yo lo habíamos hecho pero como yo no sabía nada, pues le dije que con toda seguridad habrías sido tú porque era raro que a otro se le ocurriera hacer lo tan original y chispa. (Ya has de saber cual fué la felicitación por eso no te la explico) Antier yo no vi a nadie, mas que a la Reyna, y anduvimos buscando decoraciones para el teatrito que se va a llamar TEATRO PELLO; y viendo la manera más eficaz de conseguir chamba, le mandamos un telegrama a Chole de la siguiente alambicación.

"Estimada Señorita.
Estudiantes ruegan respetuosamente se sirva concederles una entrevista.
Contestación a Pimentel 31. Srtas. A. Reyna y F. K."

Yo creo que únicamente le regalamos al telégrafo nuestro tostón

1925
8 January

Thursday 8 January 1925

My Alex (insured property): I've been terribly sad because you're sick, and I would have liked to have been at your side the whole time, but since that can't be I just have to grin and bear it till you get better, which I hope will be very soon.

These days in the mornings I've been going to the old man's office, and in the afternoon I was at your pal Reynilla's, as you will doubtless have guessed when you received the little package I sent you with the Reynis's maid, right?

Last night the only one I saw was Salas who told me you had wished him happy New Year in a very extravagant and amusing way, and he even thought that you and I had done it together, but since I didn't know anything about it I told him it must surely have been you, because it would be odd that anyone else had thought of doing it in such an original and clever way. (You must already know what the greeting was so I don't need to explain.)

The day before yesterday I really didn't see anyone except Reyna and we went looking for decorations for the little theatre that is going to be called TEATRO PELLO, and trying in the most effective way to get some work we sent Chole a telegram of the following extravagance:

> Dear Miss:
> Students respectfully beg you to be so good as to grant them an interview.
> Reply to Pimentel 31. Misses A. Reyna and F.K.

I think we just gave away our 50 centavo piece to the telegraph operator, but the important thing is to try. On Monday at 8:30 in the morning we're going to start taking classes in shorthand and typing at the Oliver so that we're not so inept in that matter, but even so I'm sadder than anything because I just can't get

Frida Kahlo, *Portrait of Alejandro Gómez Arias*, 1928, oil on canvas, 61.5 × 41 cm

any work quickly and time is flowing like water. The Güera Olaguibel is probably going to work in *[the newspaper]* El Globo de Palavicini and the other day when I bumped into her on the bus she told me she was being offered a job in the Education Library, but she needed a letter of recommendation from one of those big shots, and if I could get one she would let me have the job because she's almost sure to have a job at El Globo, and that's why I want to see Chole or whoever the hell I can find who will do me a favour. They pay 4 or 4.50, which doesn't seem bad to me at all, but first of all I need to know something about typing and scribbling. So that's how it is, you see how dense your friend is!

But right now the only thing I want is for you to get better and all the rest is in 5th and 6th place, because in 1st to 4th place is that you get better and that you love me, etc., etc. I must have bored you to death with so many things, so I'll say goodbye for now, but I'll come around to see you soon (Song of the Woodpecker). Write to Chong Lee, he's been asking me to say hello to you in my letters, and write to me too, or if you're all better tell me when you're going to go out so I can see you, because you can see I'm a real cry-baby and if I don't see you I won't be able to keep myself from weeping like Saint Peter.

Get better very, very soon and think about me a little bit, that's what your sister (girlfriend, buddy, wife) wants.
Frieda

[At the top of the 2nd page: on the left a drawing of a heart with a bed and one person lying in the bed with an arrow pointing to it that says 'you' and a person standing with an arrow that says 'me'. In the centre, a drawing of a doll and on the right:] Answer me right away in letters of condolence because I like them a lot.

7-25-925.
Aniv. del 27º mes.

Mi Alex:

No te escribí antes porque desde el miércoles en la noche estoy mala, pero no te imaginas las ganas que tengo de verte o cuando menos de que me hubieras escrito, como me dijiste, pero nada de árboles, tú nada más prometes y nunca cumples, lo que me prueba que tú, que según supongo has estado bueno, no has tenido un solo momento para escribirle a tu novia. Con toda seguridad la quieres una barbaridad verdad? Y luego no quieres que te diga que ya te olvidaste por completo de Miguel........ pero yo creo que vas a procurar que verme aunque sea un poquito, verdad mi Alex?

Cuéntame algo nuevo de Mexico, de tu life y de todo lo que tú quieras contarme pues ya sabes que aquí no hay más que pasto y pasto, indios e indios y jacales y jacales y .... de hoy no sabes, así es que aunque no lo creas estoy aburridísima con "a" de Alcancía. Me escribió la Reyna invitándome a una excursión con Delille y Ana María y decía que Uds también irían pero no le he podido contestar y de todas maneras no me dejarían ir, pues como supieron lo de la Centella, que les cayó a los de la Preparatoria, están re escamadas.

Ayer fué santo de la Kitty y vinieron una bola de escuincles a verla, así es que le tienes que dar su abrazo cuando la veas eh?

Mi Alex a ver si puedes venir el martes a las 6 pues creo que antes no tendré pretexto para salir tardecito y ya ves que en la tarde es una plancha con p. de penitente pues toda la manada vé.

Escríbeme, no seas tan de atiro, siquiera un momentito de 10 minutos piensa en tu chamaca que te adora de veras con todo su corazón — Cuando vengas por lo que más quieras tráeme algo para leer porque cada día estoy más bruta. (Dispensa lo pelada que soy) tu cuate Friedricha

1925
25 July

25 July 1925
21-month anniv.

My Alex: I didn't write to you sooner because I've been ill since Wednesday night, but you can't imagine how much I want to see you or wish you had at least written to me like you said you would, but nothing. You always make promises and never keep them, which proves to me that you, who are presumably in good health, haven't had a single moment to write to your girlfriend – I bet you love her a whole lot, don't you? And then you don't want me to tell you that you've already completely forgotten about Miguel... but I think you're going to try and love me even if it's just a little, right my Alex?

Tell me something new about Mexico, your life, and anything you want to tell me because you know that here there is nothing but grass and more grass, Indians and more Indians, huts and more huts and... nothing else, that's how it is even if you don't believe it, I am so bored with a capital B. Reyna wrote to me to invite me on a trip with Delille and Ana María and she said that you were going too, but I haven't been able to reply, and anyway I won't be allowed to go because *[my parents]* heard about the lightning that struck the kids from the preparatory school, so they're being really cautious.

Yesterday was Kitty's saint's day and a whole load of girls came to see her, so you'll have to give her a hug when you see her, alright?

My Alex, see if you can come on Tuesday at 6 because before then I won't have an excuse to go out and as you know, in the afternoon it's hotter than an iron in hell so everyone will notice. Write to me, don't be so bad, even just for 10 minutes, think of your girl who truly adores you with all her heart – *[Drawing of a heart.]*

When you come, for goodness sake bring me something to read because I am getting more stupid every day. (Excuse me for being so rude.)
Your buddy
Frieducha

1925
13 October

Tuesday 13 October 1925 *[The tram accident had happened on 17 September.]*

Alex of my life:
You know better than anyone how sad I have been in this filthy hospital, since you must imagine it, and also I suppose the boys have told you. Everyone tells me not to despair; but they don't know what it is for me to be bedridden for three months, which is what I need to be, after having been a first-class stray cat all my life, but what's there to do, since la pelona[4] *[Drawing of a skull and crossbones.]* didn't carry me away. Don't you think?

Imagine the anguish I felt not knowing how you were that day and the day after; after I had been operated on, Salas and Olmedo arrived; it was certainly good to see them! Especially Olmedo, you have no idea; I asked them about you and they told me what had happened was very painful, but not serious and you don't know how I've cried for you, my Alex, at the same time as for my pains, because I'm telling you during the first treatments my hands felt like paper and I was sweating from the pain of the wound… which went straight through my hip and out the front; I was all but left a ruin for the rest of my life and almost died, but now it's all over, one wound has closed, and the doctor says he will close the other one. They must have explained to you what I have, right? And it's all a question of lots of time for the fracture in my pelvis to heal, and for my elbow to get better and for the other small wounds in my foot to heal…

7

pastillas y un balero como el que perdimos el otro día. Porque te aliviaras muy pronto me estaría otro quince días en este Hospital.

Dime como está tu mamacita linda y Alice.

Tu cuate que se ha quedado como nido de bolita.

Friducha

(Sentí mucho el paragüitas chiquitito)

¡La vida comienza mañana — — — —

— TE ADORO —

13 October 1925

A 'crowd of folk' and a 'cloud of smoke' have come to visit me, even Chucho Ríos y Valles asked about me several times by telephone and they say he came once, but I didn't see him. They said the same about Luis de la Urra but I doubt it because he also didn't come up. Nelson Furbeck said a lot of prayers for me. Fernández is still giving me some dough, and it turns out I have even more talent for drawing than before, since he says that when I get better he's going to pay me 60 a week (just empty talk, but anyway), and all the gang from the village come to visit every day and Señor Rouaix even started crying, the father, eh, don't think it was the son, and well, you can imagine how many others. Alejandro Elguezabal and Carmen Jaime also came and Salas hasn't missed a day. You don't know how grateful I am to him, as well as to Olmedo.

But I would give anything, instead of all the people from Coyoacán and instead of all the old women who also come, if you came one day. I think the day I see you Alex, I'm going to kiss you, there's no help for it; now I see more than ever how I love you with all my soul and I won't trade you for anyone; you see how suffering something is always worthwhile.

In addition to having been pretty mangled physically, even though as I told Salas I don't think it's too serious, I have suffered very much emotionally, since you know how ill my mum was, just like my dad, and dealing them this blow hurt me more than forty wounds; just imagine, my poor little mother says she cried like a madwoman for three days, and my dad, who was getting much better, got very ill.

They have only brought my mum to see me twice since I've been here, 25 days today, which have seemed like an eternity to me, and my dad once; so I want to go home as soon as possible; but that won't be until the swelling goes down completely and all the wounds heal, so there's no chance of infection and so I don't go to… ruin. What do you think? In any case I don't think it will be longer than this week. The boys will let you know. If you can't do the miracle of showing up on Thursday, here or there, I'll be waiting for you. I'm counting the hours as I wait for you wherever, here or at home, because seeing you, the months in bed will pass much faster.

Listen, my Alex, if you can't come yet, write to me. You can't know how much your letter helped me feel better, I think I've read it twice a day since I got it and it always seems as if it were the first time I'm reading it. I have a bunch of things to tell you, but I can't write them because I'm still very weak, my head and eyes ache when I read or write a lot, but I'll tell you them soon.

Changing the subject, I'm so hungry I can't tell you… and I can't eat anything but some revolting things, so be forewarned; when you come bring me some sweets and a balero[5] like the one we lost the other day. For you to get better soon I would stay another fifteen days in this hospital.

Tell me how is your lovely little mother and Alice *[Alejandro's sister, Alicia]*.

Your buddy who has grown as thin as a rake.
[Drawing of a stick figure.] Friducha

(I was very sad about the little parasol!)
[Drawing of a crying face.]
Life begins tomorrow…!

– I adore you –

If you want, tomorrow, Friday, I can see you in the evening at the little tree... to give ourselves up to love...

1925
26 November

26 November 1925

My beloved Alex: I can't explain to you everything that I'm going through now, because can you believe that my mother had a seizure and I was with her, because Cristina was out when you came, and the wretched maid told you I wasn't home, and I am so angry that you cannot imagine; I wanted to see you, to be with you for a while alone as we haven't been for so long. It makes me want to say all the bad words I know to that damned, wretched maid. I went out to call to you from the balcony and sent her to look for you, but she didn't find you, so I had no choice but to cry out of pure anger and suffering....

Believe me Alex, I want you to come see me because I'm in over my head and I can't help but hold on, because it would be worse if I despaired, don't you think? I want you to come and talk to me like before, to forget everything and to come see me for the love of your holy mother and to tell me that you love me even if it's not true, ok? (The pen doesn't write very well with so many tears.)

I would like to tell you so many things, Alex, but I feel like crying and the only thing I can do is convince myself that you are coming.... Forgive me, but it wasn't my fault you came for nothing, my Alex.

Write to me soon.
Your dear Friducha

1926
21 August

21 August 1926

[At the top of the page, centre, an F and an A joined together and a heart with an arrow through it. On the right, two sailboats, a setting sun and a crying face.]

My Alex:

I'm not a dummy as you thought last night, because I didn't say goodbye to you, because as much as I tried, I couldn't get out at the signal. But I hope you will pardon me, no?

If you want, tomorrow, Friday, I can see you in the evening, at the little tree... to give ourselves up to love...

I will phone you at four, eh? (It is not 'he', you know?)

I need you to tell me several times... 'Don't be a cry-baby' – it's very sweet for me.

'I love you' very much. Do you believe me?

Well, I implore you to forgive me about yesterday, it was because of my mum.

Yours for ever.
Frieda
Cry-baby of Gómez Arias
Or the Virgin Lacrimorum

You haven't written to me because it was so windy last night, right?

A very strong wind. *[Illustration of Frida with her cheeks puffed out and blowing a strong wind.]*

[A circle with the words:] My mouth was here for a long time. *[Underneath the circle it says:]* I adore you Alex.

For the simpleton verbi gracia
(I charge $2.00 to illustrate letters)

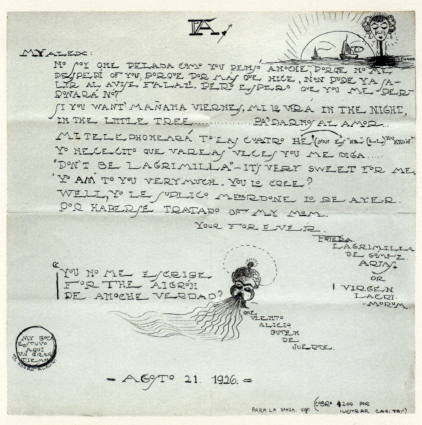

21 August 1926

Trams in Mexico City, 1912

Guillermo Kahlo (1871–1941), Frida Kahlo as a student, 1926

1927
22 April

Good Friday, 22 April 1927

My Alex: Alicia has written to me; but since 28 March neither she nor anyone else has had the slightest news of you.... There is nothing comparable to the desperation of not knowing anything about you for a month.

I'm still unwell, I'm losing a lot of weight; and the doctor decided after all to have me wear the plaster corset for three or four months, because that grooved thing, even though it's a little less bothersome than the corset, is not as effective since it's a question of being in it for months.*[...]* With the corset I'm going to suffer horribly, because I need to be immobile, and to put it on me they are going to have to hang me from my head and wait until it dries, otherwise it would be completely useless because of the warped position my spine is in, and by hanging me they are going to try to get me as straight as possible, but because of all this, and it's not the half of it, you can imagine how I will be suffering. The old doctor says the corset gives very good results when it is put on properly, but that's still to be seen, and if the devil doesn't take me they are going to put it on me on Monday in the Hospital Francés.*[...]*

1927
15 July

15 July 1927

My Alex: I still can't tell you I'm doing better, but nevertheless I feel much happier than before, I have so much hope of getting better by the time you return that you shouldn't be sad on my account for a single moment. I almost never lose hope now, and I'm very rarely a 'cry-baby'. On 9 August I will have been in this position for two months, and the doctor says they are going to take an X-ray to see how the vertebrae are, and it's almost certain that I'll only need the plaster apparatus until the 9th of

September, after that I don't know what they'll do with me. They are going to take the X-ray here at home, because I absolutely mustn't move at all. I'm on a table with little wheels so they can take me out into the sun, and you couldn't by any means imagine how bothersome it is, since I haven't moved at all for more than a month, but I'm willing to be like this for six months, if it means getting better. I guess that you'll be here at the beginning of August, right? But if you can't be here by then, I don't want you to worry, because you know I'd give anything so you'd be happy, and particularly now that you are alone, because here between us, you know how to be happy. Besides, there is no reason for you to suffer for me, everything I tell you in my letters is because I'm such a 'cry-baby' and at the end just a young girl, but it is not that much, it is fine to suffer a little, don't you think, my Alex? I'll be very happy when you come back so it is fair that things are like this now, and you are coming back, what more could I ask for? You can't imagine how marvellous it is to wait for you with the same serenity as the portrait. How much faith I have now, Alex! And you have given it all to me.

[...] Write to me a little bit more, your letters really heal me.
Alice, your little sister, is really cute.
The guys have been really good with me, I really thank them so much. And I, my Alex, the only thing I do is to love you more.

Your Friducha.

1927
22 July

22 July 1927
Day of Mary of Magdalene

My Alex:... Despite so much suffering, I think I'm getting better, it may not be true, but I already want to believe it.

Julio 15 de 1927.

Mi Alex:

Todavía no puedo decirte que sigo mejor, pero sin embargo estoy mucho más contenta que antes, tengo tanta esperanza de aliviarme para cuando tú vuelvas, que ya no debes estar triste por mí ni un solo momento, ya casi nunca me desespero, y muy pocas veces soy "lagrimilla", el día nueve de agosto, hago dos meses de estar en esta posición y dice el Dr. que me sacarán una radiografía para ver cómo están las vertebras y es casi seguro que solamente hasta el nueve de septiembre estaré con el aparato de yeso, después no sé qué harán conmigo. La radiografía me la van a tomar aquí mismo en la casa, pues no debo moverme absolutamente nada, estoy en una mesa con carretillas para que puedan sacarme al sol, y de ninguna manera podrías imaginarte, qué molesto es ésto, pues tengo ya más de un mes de no moverme para nada, pero ya estoy dispuesta a estar así seis meses, con tal de aliviarme. Yo creo que cuando vengas a principios de agosto estarás aquí ¿verdad? pero si no pudieras para entonces, quiero que no estés apenado, pues

And I, my Alex, the only thing I do is to love you more.

It's better anyway, don't you think? These four months have been a continuous pain for me, day by day, now I am almost ashamed of not having had faith, but no one can imagine how I have suffered. Your poor girlfriend! You would have carried me, as I told you when I was a girl, in one of your pockets, like the golden nugget in Velarde's poem… but now I am so big! I have grown so much since then.*[…]*

Hey, my Alex: how wonderful the Louvre must be; I'm going to learn so many things when you return.

I had to look for Nice in the atlas, because I couldn't remember where it was (I've always been a bit of a dunce) but I will never forget now… believe me.

Alex: I'm going to confess one thing: there are moments that I think you're forgetting me, but you aren't, right? You couldn't fall in love with the Mona Lisa.*[…]*

News in my house
– Maty is coming to this mansion.[6] Peace has been made.
(All the Catholic ladies – Night Watcher, Granny, Pianist, etc. – ended their days because of this anti-Catholic chance.)
– My dad is no longer in La Perla but in Uruguay 51.

Out of my house
– Chelo Navarro had a girl.
– Jack Dempsey won against Jack Sharkey in New York. What a sensation!

The revolution in Mexico:	Re-electionists
	Anti-reelectionists
Interesting candidates:	José Vasconcelos (?)
	Luis Cabrera

In my heart
– only you –

Your
Frieda

1927
2 August

2 August 1927

Alex: August has begun, and I could say that life has too if I were sure that you are coming back at the end of this month, but yesterday Bustamante told me that you are probably going to Russia, so you will stay longer....

Yesterday was Esperanza Ordoñez's saint's day, and they threw a party at my house because they don't have a piano. The boys (Salas, Mike *[Miguel Lira, poet and fellow member of The Cachucas]*, Flaquer), my sister Matilde and other boys and girls were here. I was taken to the living room in my little car and I watched everybody dance and sing. The boys had a very good time (I think).*[...]*

I was a little weepy as always. Although they now take me out every morning for four hours to take some sun, I don't feel that I've got any better, since the pains are always the same and I am very thin. But in spite of this, I want to have faith, as I told you in the other letter. If there is money this month, they will take another X-ray and I will be more certain; if not, I'm going to get up out of bed on 9 or 10 September no matter what, and then I will know whether this apparatus will help me recover or if the operation will be necessary (I'm afraid). But I will still have to wait for quite a long time to see if the absolute rest of these three months (I could almost call it martyrdom) works or not.

According to what you tell me, the Mediterranean is wonderfully blue. Will I ever get to see it? I don't think so because I have very bad luck, and my biggest dream for a long time has been to travel. I'll just be left with the melancholy of those who read travel books. I'm not reading anything now. I don't want to. I'm not studying German or doing anything but thinking of you. I must think that I'm terribly wise. And aside from departures and arrivals of steamships, in the newspaper, I only read the editorials and what's happening in Europe.

→
Frida Kahlo, *Self Portrait with Velvet Dress*, 1926, oil on canvas, 78 × 61 cm

ALEJANDRO GÓMEZ ARIAS

As for the revolution over here, we don't know anything yet; it seems that Obregón *[future president, Álvaro Obregón]* is the one, but nobody knows anything. Aside from that, there is nothing interesting. Alex, have you learnt much French? Even though my advice may be unnecessary, try to learn as much as you can, ok? *[...]*

You can't imagine with what pleasure I would give all my life just to kiss you. I think this time I have really suffered, so I must deserve it. Right?

Will it be as you say in the month of August? Will it?
Your Frieda
(I adore you)

1927
15 October

15 October 1927

My Alex: The second to last letter! Everything that I could tell you, you already know.

We've been happy every winter but none will compare to this. Life is ahead of us, it's impossible to explain to you what that means.

It's likely that I'm still unwell, but I don't know anymore. In Coyoacán the nights are amazing just like in 1923, and the sea, a symbol in my portrait, synthesizes life, my life.

You haven't forgotten me?
It would almost be unfair, don't you think?
Your Frieda

1934
12 October

12 October 1934

Alex,

The electricity went out and I stopped painting the little figures. I kept thinking about the decoration on the wall separated by another wall of wisdom. My head is full of microscopic arachnids and a large number of minute vermin. I think we'll have to build the wall in a microscopic type as well, otherwise it will be difficult to proceed with the fallacious painting. Furthermore, do you think that all the silent wisdom will fit into such a limited space? And what of booklets containing such lyrics in almost non-existent pages? That is the big problem, and it's up to you to solve it architecturally because, as you say, I cannot organize anything within the big realité without going straight to the crash, or I have to hang clothes from the air, or place that which is distant in a dangerous and fatal proximity. You'll save everything with the ruler and the compass.

Do you know that I've never seen a jungle? How can I paint a jungle background with vermin? Anyway, I'll do what I can and if it doesn't please you, you can proceed to the certain and effective dismantling of what has already been built and painted. But it will take so long to conclude that we'll never have time to even think about the demolition.

I've not yet been able to organize the parade of tarantulas and the other beings, because I'm thinking that everything will be stuck to the first of infinite layers that such a wall must have.

It's done me such good to see you that I haven't been able to tell you. Now I dare to write it because you're not here, and because it's a letter written in the usual winter. I don't know if you'll believe it, but it is so, and I can't write to you without telling you.

Tomorrow I'll talk to you, and I would like you to write to me one day, even if it's just three words. I don't know why I'm asking you this, but I know that I need you to write to me. Will you?

BARBIZON · PLAZA · HOTEL
101 west 58th street · · · central park south · · new york

Alex,

El nuevo día de mi exposición te quiero platicar aunque sea éste poquito.

Todo se arregló a las mil maravillas y realmente me cargo una suerte lépera. La manada de aquí me tiene gran cantidad de cariño y son todos de un amable elevado. El prefacio de A. Breton no quiso Levy traducirlo y es lo único que me parece un poco ajenas pues tiene un aspecto medio

1 November 1938

1938
1 November

[Written on stationery from the Barbizon Plaza Hotel, on the day of the opening of her exhibition at the Julien Levy Gallery in New York, 1 November 1938.]

Alex,
On the very same day as my exhibition, I want to chat with you even if just a little.

Everything worked out marvellously and I have been ridiculously lucky. The gang here has great affection for me and they are all very kind. Levy didn't want to translate A. Breton's preface and it is the only thing that seems a bit unfortunate to me as it looks rather pretentious, but it can't be fixed now! What do you think? The gallery is great and they have arranged the paintings really well. Have you seen *Vogue*? There are 3 copies, one in colour – which I think is the best – and something will also appear in *Life* this week.

I saw 2 wonderful pieces in a private collection, a Piero della Francesca with the largest teeth in the world, and a little Greco, which is the tiniest I've seen but the sweetest of them all. I am sending you copies. Write to me some day if you think of me. I'll be here for another 2 or 3 weeks. I love you so much.

Frida

[Along the right side of the page and around the top:] Say hello to Mike and Rebe from me. Aurea is here and is more bearable now than before.

1946
30 June

New York, 30 June 1946

Alex darling,
They don't let me write much, but this is just to tell you I swallowed the big operation. Three weeks ago they proceeded to the cut-cut of bones. And these doctors are so marvellous and my body so full of vitality, that today they proceeded to get me up on my poor feet for two short minutes. I myself no lo believo. The first two weeks were all suffering and tears, for I wouldn't wish the pain on anybody; it was so piercing and dreadful, but this week the pain has decreased and with the help of the little pills I've more or less survived. I have two whopping scars on my back in this shape. *[Drawing, as shown left.]* From there they proceeded to yank out a piece of my pelvis to graft it on to my column, which is where the scar is least hair-raising and straightest. Five vertebra were damaged but now they're going to be fine.

The nuisance is that it takes a long time for the bone to grow and re-adjust itself, and I still have six weeks left in bed until they release me from the hospital and I can flee this horrible city for my beloved Coyoacán. How are you? Please write to me and send me some little book; please don't forget me. How is your Mummy? Alex, don't leave me all alone, alone in this foul hospital, write to me. Cristi is bored out of her mind and we're roasting in the heat. There's a terrible lot of heat and we don't know what to do. What's new in Mexico? What's happening with everybody there?

Tell me about everyone and above all, about yourself.
Your F.

I send you so much affection and lots of kisses. I got your letter, it cheered me up a lot! Don't forget me.

New York. Junio 30/46

Alex darling,

No me dejan escribir mucho pero es solo para decirte que ya pasé the big trago operatorio. Hace tres weeks que procedieron al corte y corte de huesores. Y es tan maravilloso éste medicamen, y tan lleno de vitalidad mi body, que hoy ya procedieron al paren en mis puper feet por dos minutillos, pero yo misma no lo belivo. Las dos first semanas fueron de gran sufrimiento y lágrimas pues los dolores no se los deseo a nobody — son buten de estridentes y malignos, pero ya en esta semana

30 June 1946

LETTERS TO:

Diego Rivera

An All-Consuming Love

*You are now my life itself,
and nothing and no one
can change me.*

Diego Rivera (1886–1957) was one of several artists commissioned by the Mexican government to paint murals in the former San Ildefonso College in Mexico City in 1922. The building then housed the National Preparatory School, where Frida began studying that same year. She encountered Diego and joked to her friends that she would one day have the muralist's baby.[7]

Six years later, Frida sought out Diego to ask his opinion of her artwork. In the intervening years, she had experienced the devastating trolley accident, the disintegration of her relationship with Alejandro and had turned to painting to pass the time during her convalescence but also with the hope that she would one day be able to make a living from art. She looked to Diego for confirmation that she was good enough and should continue to paint. Diego was charmed by Frida, encouraged her and took her under his wing.

They were married in August 1929. Diego was 20 years older, had lived in Europe for a decade and had two failed marriages. He was a well-known painter receiving high-profile commissions and was prominent in the Mexican Communist Party. Frida was young, inexperienced, but clever and artistically talented. Diego was unfaithful from the beginning; he often said that fidelity was a bourgeois notion,[8] and Frida tried to be open-minded about his constant philandering. It saddened her and made her jealous, but she tolerated it and enjoyed flirtations of her own.

In 1934, Diego became involved with Frida's younger sister, Cristina. Frida was devastated. She moved out of the home they shared and tried to forge a life for herself separate from her husband. However, she missed him and their life together, eventually deciding to forgive him and her sister. Frida and Diego resumed their relationship, but from that time on,

Diego Rivera at work, 1948

Diego, Frida and their dog, Mexico City, 1940s

she focused more on her artwork and gained recognition as an artist in her own right. She also had more meaningful, passionate love affairs of her own. In 1939, following Frida's exhibitions in New York and Paris, Diego requested a divorce. She was again despondent, but they remarried the following year (see p. 66). This time the marriage would last, but Frida remained at her family home in Coyoacán and Diego maintained a studio in San Ángel, where he stayed much of the time.

Throughout the course of their tumultuous 27-year-long relationship, they both had many affairs. Frida became resigned to Diego's ways, writing 'Perhaps it is expected that I should lament how I have suffered living with a man like Diego. But I do not think the banks of a river suffer because they let the river flow, nor does the earth suffer because of the rains, nor does the atom suffer for letting its energy escape. To my way of thinking, everything has its natural compensation.'[9]

However inconstant they were in their romantic relationship, Frida and Diego were unfailingly supportive of each other as artists. They had great respect for the other's work, and inspired, praised and encouraged one another. After Frida died, Diego said: 'Too late now I realize that the most wonderful part of my life has been my love for Frida.'[10] Diego helped cement Frida's legacy by creating a trust leaving her family home and the museum he called Anahuacalli ('house surrounded by water'), along with their contents and artwork, to the Mexican people.

1932
10 September

10 September 1932

Although you tell me that you see yourself as very ugly when you look in the mirror with your short hair, I don't believe it. I know how handsome you are anyway and the only thing that I regret is not to be there to kiss you and take care of you, and even if I would sometimes bother you with my grumbling, I adore you, my Diego. I feel as though I've left my child with no one and that you need me.... I cannot live without my cute little boy. The house without you is nothing. Everything without you seems horrible to me. I am in love with you more than ever, and each moment more and more.

I send you all my love.
Your niña chiquititita *[little girl]*

1935
23 July

23 July 1935

A certain letter I happened to see, in a certain jacket, belonging to a certain gentleman, coming from a certain lady from distant and damned Germany. I think it must be the lady that Willi Valentiner *[art critic and museum director]* sent here to have fun and with 'scientific', 'artistic' and 'archaeological' purposes.... It made me angry and, to tell you the truth, jealous.*[...]*

Why do I have to be so stubborn and obstinate as to not understand that the letters, the liaisons with petticoats, the female teachers of... English, the gypsy models, the assistants with 'good intentions', the disciples interested in the 'art of painting' and the plenipotentiary emissaries sent from distant places are just simply jokes, and that deep inside, you and I love each other a lot? Even if we experience endless affairs, cracks in the doors, mentions of our mothers, and international

pag. 391   Favor de devolver
                                    39
sista María
A man wrote that he was trying
to arrange an exposition in Minne-
apolis
" te extraño muchísimo y la chaparra
también."

Letter 23 July 1935. to same place.

"cierta carta, que ví de casualidad,
en cierto vaso, de cierto señor, y
que procedía de cierta damisela de la
lejana y pinche alemania, y que
me imagino que debe ser la dama que
Willi Valentiner tuvo a bien mandar
aquí a vacilar con intenciones
'científicas', 'artísticas' y
'arqueológicas'... me dió mucho
coraje y a decir verdad celos..."
— . — . — . — . — . —
¿Porqué seré tan mula y rejega de no
entender que las cartas, los líos con
enaguas, las profesoras de... inglés,
las modelos gitanas, las ayudantes
de 'buena voluntad', las discípulas

23 July 1935

All this anger has simply made me understand better that I love you more than my own skin

complaints, don't we always love each other? I think that what is happening is that I am a little stupid and a fool because all these things have happened and have repeated themselves during the seven years that we've lived together. All this anger has simply made me understand better that I love you more than my own skin, and that even though you don't love me as much, you love me a little anyway – don't you? If this isn't true, I'll always be hopeful that it could be, and that's enough for me....

Love me a little. I adore you.
Frieda

1939
9 January

9 January 1939

My child,
Yesterday when we spoke on the phone I noticed you seemed a bit sad and I've been worried about you. I would like to receive a letter from you before I leave with details about Coyoacán and how things are in general. Here three articles have appeared in the news about the old man and the general, I'm sending them so you can see how stupid they are in this damn town, they say that Lombardo *[Vicente Lombardo Toledano, labour leader and politician]* is a furious Trotskyist, etc., etc.

You know I'm going to spend this last week at Mary's house. Last night she came to get me, because David wants me to rest a lot and sleep very well before I embark on the journey, because the damn flu made me terribly ill and I feel completely face down and stupid. I miss you so much, my sweetheart, that there are moments when I want to go to Mexico more than anything, and I was already giving up last week about going to Paris, but as you say, it will perhaps be the last chance I have to go. I'm going to bite the bullet and go. In March I'll be back in Mexico

because I don't plan to stay more than a month in Paris.*[...]*
I was so glad that you liked the portrait I did of Goodyear
*[founder and first president of the Museum of Modern Art, New
York]*, he's delighted and when I return, he wants one of
Katharine Cornell *[American actor]* and one of his daughter, but
it will be in October when you come with me, because I don't
want to spend any longer without you. I already need you like
air to breathe and it's a real sacrifice that I make by going to
Europe, because what I want is my child near me.

I don't know what the Bretons are planning because they
haven't written to me again at all, they didn't even respond to
the cable I sent them last week. I think they're going to wait for
me in Cherbourg or wherever the ship stops, because I don't
know what the heck I would do alone in those lands that I don't
even know in the slightest.

My dear, don't play too much with Fulang *[their pet monkey]*
because you know what he did to your eye, it's better just to see
him from a distance but he'd better not seriously hurt you one
day because I'd kill him.*[...]*

My dear boy, tell Kitty to take care of your clothes, to keep
everything clean and to call the 'hairdresser' when you need him.
Don't forget to bathe and take good care of yourself. Don't forget
that I love you more than my life, that I miss you more and more
every minute. Be good, and even if you have fun, never stop loving
me even a little. I'll write to you about Paris as often as I can, but
don't give me the pain of not hearing a word from you. Even if
they're very small letters or cards, let me know how your health is.

The painting of the dead woman *[The Suicide of Dorothy Hale]*
is coming along well. The only thing I can't get right is the space
between the figures, and the building looks like one of those
square chimneys, and it looks very short. Every day I'm more
convinced of how poor I am at drawing and how stupid I feel

when I want to add some distance to a painting. What I would give to see what you're doing now, what you're painting, to be close to you and to sleep with you in our little room on the bridge; I miss your laugh, your voice, your hands, your eyes, even your anger, everything, my child, all of you, you are now my life itself, and nothing and no one can change me.

These days I'm waiting for your letter that you promised me in the telegram and by phone. Tell me why you felt sad, tell me everything, tell me if you want me to go to you and I'll send Paris and everyone to hell. I send you millions and millions of kisses and all my heart.

Your little girl.
Friduchin

1939
19 August

19 August 1939

My child,
Ten years ago today we were married, you surely don't remember that day, nor the date, nor anything about it. I do. I'm sending you these flowers and in each one a pile of kisses and the same affection we have had all our lives.

This morning I remembered the time I woke up and I said: '¡Zocalo! I'm very late for school.' (20 August 1929)

I adore you
Frida

Diego in his studio at San Ángel, 1940

Diego and Frida remarry at San Francisco City Hall, 1940

1940
11 June

11 June 1940
Letter-report to Diego Rivera

Diego, my dear child,
I received your letter yesterday and I wanted to write to you right away, but, as I have so many things to tell you and I arrived very tired from San Ángel, I fell like a log and I waited to write to you today more calmly. Your letter pleased me very much; the only good thing that's happened to me in days and days is receiving your letters. I'll never be able to explain to you the joy that it gives me to know that you are well outside of all this shitty mess. As soon as they knew that you were on the 'other side' things changed immediately, as you can imagine.[11] *[...]*

My dear, Montezuma's treasure is secured in my possession. I personally packed the characters one by one, counting them and separating them according to their origin.[12] There were 57 large wooden crates just for the clay pieces, and we carried the stone separately. I left out the most precious and fragile things, and in a few days I'll send you the exact list of how much you have. I think it's best to leave them packed as they are until further orders from you, as they're much safer and easier to transport that way. At your house I left only the stone ones that were in the garden, numbered, and in the care of Mary Eaton. She brought me your drawings, photographs, all kinds of papyri, etc. Everything is in my jurisdiction. I left only bare furniture in San Ángel, the house swept and cleaned, the garden arranged, etc. So I think that on that side you should be completely at ease. They can kill me now, I won't let them steal your things.

All of your things make me think of you and I suffer horribly, especially the things that you love most: the treasure, the mask with the snout and many others, but for now I just have to be strong. I'm glad I was able to help you to the best of my ability, although I didn't have the honour of doing as much for you as Miss Irene Bohus and Mrs Goddard! According to your statements to the press, they were the heroines and the only ones deserving of your gratitude. Don't think that I'm telling you this out of personal jealousy or for glory, but I just want to remind you that there is someone else who also deserves your gratitude, especially for not expecting any reward, whether journalistic or otherwise…, and that is Arturo Arámburo. Although he's not the husband of any world 'star', nor does he have 'artistic genius', he does have his balls in place and has done the unspeakable to help you, especially you, as well as Cristina and I who were absolutely alone; I think he deserves huge consideration. People like him always remain unknown, but at least I know that they're worth more than all the world stardom of disgusting careerists, and all the young painters with supernatural talent. That talent is always in direct proportion to the temperature of their bottoms. You know what I mean. And now, better than before, I understand your statements and Miss (?) Bohus's 'insistence' on meeting me. Nothing makes me happier than having told her to go to hell. According to a very kind letter from you to Goodyear, you invite her to be your assistant in San Francisco. I think the matter is already arranged, hopefully she'll learn fresco in her free time, after riding horses in the mornings, and devoting herself to the 'sport' of training slugs. To Mrs Goddard, give my most repeated thanks for her timely and magnificent cooperation, and above all for her punctuality and 'coincidence' at the time of taking the plane. She must be clairvoyant, because Ch. assures me that he did not go with you and that he did not know anything about your departure. If I wasn't trusted until the last moment to be told certain things, she enjoyed the privilege of absolute trust, there must have been reasons for that. Unfortunately, I was completely unaware of my classification among the sly and suspicious people. Now, too late, I realize some things. That's how it goes in this life!

In any case, in what was entrusted to me, I have tried to comply to the letter. *[An account of payments made and a lengthy discussion of finances is omitted.]*

→
Frida Kahlo, *Diego and I*, 1949, oil on canvas, 75.9 × 62.9 cm

I've suffered the unspeakable and a lot more now that you're gone.

Now I'll tell you about myself, as you requested in your letter. I don't think I need to tell you much because you already know my situation very well. I've suffered the unspeakable and a lot more now that you're gone. In these last days, weeks, that is, I haven't painted and I think that another few will pass until I feel better and start again. Since the months are passing quickly, I don't think I'll be able to do the exhibition in New York in January. I wrote to Levy but he hasn't answered, I don't even know what happened to my painting *The Wounded Table* that Miguel took to deliver to Levy. I don't have any news about the exhibition. What you say in your letter is very kind but very doubtful because unfortunately, I don't think anyone's interested in my work. There's not much reason for them to take an interest and much less for me to believe it.

I was hoping that the Guggenheim would be arranged for this month, but I haven't had any response, and no hope. When I heard that you had in your possession the first self-portrait that I painted this year (or last, I don't remember) and which I naively took to Misrachi's house *[art dealer and gallery owner in Mexico City]* so that he could send it to the buyer… and when I saw that it hadn't even been unpacked, you and Misrachi having deceived me with a sweet and caring lie. I could have pardoned in part the deceit since according to your story you exchanged it for one of yours because you didn't want to be without my portrait; I became aware of many things. The painting of the hair, the one of the butterflies, and this one, your marvellous painting of the sleeping girl, which I loved so much and you sold to Kaufman so that he could give me the money, has been all that has sustained me this year and last. Your money, that is. I've continued to live off you, with illusions that it was otherwise. In conclusion, I've realized that I haven't done anything but fail. As a girl I wanted to become a doctor and a bus crushed me. I lived with you for ten years and it turns out that I've just been a bother and annoyance to you. I started to paint and it turns out it's only for myself and so you'll buy it, knowing that no one else would buy it. Now that I would give my life to save you, it turns out that others are the real 'saviours'. Maybe I'm just thinking this way because I feel ruined and alone, and above all exhausted from inner fatigue. I don't think that sun, proper eating, or medicine will cure me, but I'll wait a little longer to see what this state of mind is dependent on. The bad thing is that I think I already know, and there's no remedy. I'm no longer interested in New York, much less now with all the Irenes, etc. there. I don't have the least desire to work, or the ambition I would like to have. I'll keep painting for you to see my things. I don't want exhibitions or anything. I'll pay what I owe with painting, and after that even if I have to eat shit I'll do exactly as I wish when I wish. The only thing that is left me is to have your things close to me, and the hope that I'll see you again, that's sufficient to keep living.

The only thing that I ask is that you don't deceive me about anything, there's no reason for it. Write to me whenever you can, try not to work too much now that you've started the fresco, take care of your eyes, don't live alone so that there's someone to watch out for you, and whatever you do, whatever happens, know that I will always adore you.

Frida

Let me know what you need from here so I can send it to you. The children and Cristi send their love.

I'll send you the other receipts and clippings.

I beg you not to lose track of this letter because I found all the others I've written to you in a pile among other messages from Irene and other whores.

Say hello to Ralph and Ginette and Dr Eloesser, and all the good friends from San Francisco.

1940
10 July

10 July 1940

[Excerpt from a 16-page letter, after explaining her doctor's analysis of her condition and treatment.]

I've followed all the doctor's instructions and I still feel as bad as before I went to see him, completely screwed, exhausted. I've lost about 5 kilos in the past two months. I don't sleep, and all day I feel like bawling. I wish I could disappear already from this damned planet. Ever since you've been gone, everything has lost its colour. I've suffered so much that no one, not even you, could imagine it. Everything, life itself, from a leaf on a tree to a mountain, every moment, all the colours, all the shapes, every single thing is linked to you.

I received a very 'kind' rejection letter from the Guggenheim. From what I've read and heard about the exhibition at the Modern Art Museum, my painting fell flat, the comments are that it is too 'bloody' and sad, and I don't know what the hell people want an idiot like me to paint with my bitter and bloody character. Nickolas Muray sent me a few dollars so that I could send him some paintings, but he tells me in his last letter not to paint such gloomy and personal things, pelvises, hearts, etc. What the hell does he want me to paint? Angels and seraphim playing the violin?

I know that no one can like my painting... only you... what could interest them in my paintings, not the content, not the painting itself, not a damn, I don't think they're so stupid as to worry right now about hanging this type of art in their houses, these kinds of things that are personal and according to them 'morbid'. In reality, they are quite right. What the hell do they care if I have a lameness complex, or if I'm in love with you, or if I imagine having huge forests on my skin?

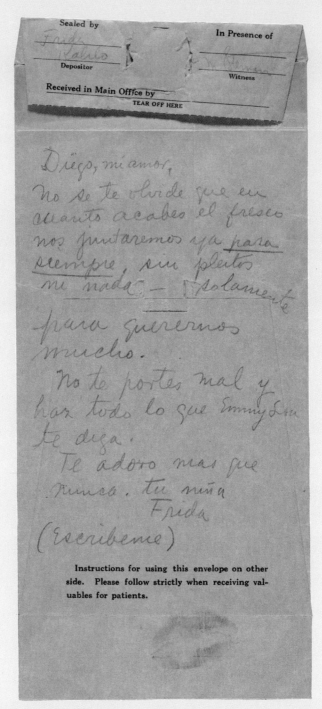

Diego, mi amor,
No se te olvide que en cuanto acabes el fresco nos juntaremos ya para siempre, sin pleitos ni nada — solamente para querernos mucho.
No te portes mal y haz todo lo que Emmy Lou te diga.
Te adoro mas que nunca. tu niña
Frida
(Escribeme)

1940

1940

[Written on an envelope.]

Diego, my love,
Remember that once you finish the fresco we will be together forever, without arguments or anything, only to love one another. Behave yourself and do everything that Emmy Lou tells you. I adore you more than ever. Your girl
Frida (Write me).

Undated diary entry

Diego.
Truth is so great that I wouldn't like to speak, or sleep, or hear, or love. To feel enclosed, with no fear of blood, outside time and magic, within your own fear, and your great anguish, and in the very beating of your heart. All this madness, if I asked it of you, I know, in your silence, there is only confusion. I ask you for violence, in the nonsense, and you, you give me grace, your light and your warmth. I'd like to paint you, but there are no colours, because there are so many, in my confusion, the tangible form of my great love.
F.

[Crossed out:] Today Diego kissed me.
Every moment, he is my child, my born child, every moment, every day, of myself.

Undated diary entry

Diego:
Nothing compares to your hands, nothing like the green-gold of your eyes. My body is filled with you for days and days. You are the mirror of the night. The violent flash of lightning. The dampness of the earth. The hollow of your armpits is my shelter,

my fingers touch your blood. All my joy is to feel life spring from your flower-fountain that mine keeps to fill all the paths of my nerves, which are yours.

——

Leaves, blades, cupboards, sparrow
I sell it all for nothing. I do not believe
in illusion – You smoke horribly (a horror).
Smoke. Marx. Life. The great
Joker. Nothing has a name.
I don't look at shapes. The paper
Love. Wars. Tangled hair. Pitchers.
Claws. Submerged spiders. Lives
In alcohol. Children are the days and here it stopped.

Undated diary entry

Auxochrome – Chromophore. Diego.
She who wears the colour.
He who sees the colour.
Since the year 1922.

Until all the days. Now in 1944. After all the hours lived. The vectors continue in their original direction. Nothing stops them. With no more knowledge than live emotion. With no other wish than to go on until they meet. Slowly. With great unease, but with the certainty that all is guided by the 'golden section'. There is cellular arrangement. There is movement. There is light. All centres are the same. Madness does not exist. We are the same as we were and as we will be. Not counting on stupid destiny.

My Diego:
Mirror of the night
Your eyes green swords inside my flesh. Waves between our hands.

→
Frida Kahlo, *Diego and Frida 1929–1944*, 1944, oil on masonite, 12.3 × 7.4 cm

Frida and Diego in his studio, 1934

All of you in a space full of sounds – in the shade and in the light. You will be called AUXOCHROME, the one who captures colour. I, CHROMOPHORE – the one who gives colour.

You are all the combinations of numbers. Life. My wish is to understand lines, form, shades, movement. You fill and I receive. Your word moves through all of space and reaches my cells, which are my stars, then goes to yours, which are my light.

[At bottom left of the page, written sideways:] Ghosts.

Auxochrome – Chromophore
It was the thirst of many years retained in our body. Words in chains, which we could not say except on the lips of a dream. Everything was surrounded by the verdant miracle of the landscape of your body. Upon your form, the eyelashes of the flowers respond to my touch, the murmur of rivers. All the fruits were in the juice of your lips, the blood of the pomegranate, the

stretch of the mamey and the virtuous pineapple. I pressed you against my chest and the wonder of your form penetrated all my blood through the tips of my fingers.

Fragrance of oak essence, memories of walnut, green breath of ash tree. Horizons and landscapes = I traced them with a kiss. Oblivion of words will form the exact language to understand the gazes of our closed eyes. = You are present, intangible and you are the whole universe that I form in the space of my room. Your absence springs trembling in the ticking of the clock, in the pulse of light; your breath through the mirror. From you to my hands, I roam your entire body, and I am with you for a minute and I am with myself for a moment. And my blood is the miracle, which runs in the vessels of the air from my heart to yours.

THE WOMAN
THE MAN

The verdant miracle of the landscape of my body becomes in you all of nature. I traverse it in flight caressing the rounded hills with my fingertips, my hands penetrate the drunken valleys anxious to possess and I'm enveloped in the embrace of gentle branches, green and cool. I penetrate the sex of the entire earth, her heat sears me and my entire body is rubbed by the freshness of the tender leaves. Her dew is the sweat of an ever-new lover.

It's not love, or tenderness, or affection, it's life itself, my life, that I found when I saw it in your hands, in your mouth and in your breasts. I have the taste of almonds from your lips in my mouth. Our worlds have never gone outside. Only one mountain can know the core of another mountain.

For a few moments, your presence floats as if wrapping my whole being in an anxious wait for morning. I notice that I'm with you. In this instant still full of sensations, my hands are sunk in oranges, and my body feels surrounded by your arms.

Page 113 from Frida's diaries, 1944–54

[Written in the left margin:] For my Diego,
The silent life-giver of worlds, what is most important is the non-illusion. Morning breaks, the friendly reds, the big blues, hands full of leaves, noisy birds, fingers in hair, pigeons' nests, a rare understanding of human struggle, simplicity of the senseless song, the folly of the wind in my heart = don't let them rhyme, girl! = sweet xocolatl of ancient Mexico, storm in the blood that comes in through the mouth – convulsion, omen, laughter and teeth, fine pearl needles, for some gift on a seventh of July, I ask for it, I get it, I sing, sang, I'll sing from now on our magic-love.

1947
8 December

8 December 1947

Child of my eyes,
You know what I would like to give you today and always.
If it were in my hands, it would already be yours.
The least I can offer you is to be with you in everything…
my heart.

Your girl,
Fisita

Undated note

Child of my eyes,
I have gone out. Here, I leave you many kisses. Rest well and for all the world don't stay up late. Eat well, and I will see you here around 10 or 11.

Your girl,
Fisita

LETTERS TO:

Nickolas Muray

An Intense Romance

To you, my loveliest Nick, all my heart, blood and all my being. I adore you.

Nick and Frida in Coyoacán, 1939

Hungarian-born Nickolas Muray (1892–1965) immigrated to the United States in 1913. He worked as an engraver before opening his own photography studio in New York City's Greenwich Village in 1920. He soon became a well-known celebrity portrait photographer and was a pioneer in colour photography. Nick met Frida through their mutual friends Miguel and Rosa Covarrubias, who had homes in New York and Mexico.

Frida's first letter to Nick is dated 31 May 1931 and is partly in Hungarian. In the following years, Nick travelled to Mexico frequently, staying with Miguel and Rosa, and visiting Frida. Their relationship was at its most intense between 1937 and 1938 when he helped her to prepare for her exhibitions in New York and Paris, and she spent time with him in New York. Her letters to him from Paris are effusive in their expressions of love, though she made it clear that Diego would always be foremost in her affections. She signed many of her letters to him with the pseudonym Xóchitl, which means 'flower' in the Náhuatl language, and their relationship was likely the inspiration for her painting *Flower of Life* (1938), which depicts a flower with strong sexual imagery.

Although Nick hoped for more with Frida, it became clear that she would never leave Diego. When Frida returned to New York following her stay in Paris, she found Nick involved with someone else, and she retreated to Mexico. Soon after her return, Diego asked for a divorce – possibly because he had learned about her affair with Nick. Frida and Nick continued their correspondence, and Nick sent her money on various occasions during her divorce. Frida remained devoted to Diego and after their remarriage, her relationship with Nick dissipated, although they would remain friends until her death.

Nick took many of the most iconic photos of Frida, including *Frida with Magenta Rebozo* (1939; see p. 103). Besides being a renowned photographer, he was also a pilot and a champion fencer, competing in the Olympics twice.

1931
31 May

31 May 1931

Nick,
[In Hungarian:]
I love you like an angel
You are a Lily of the valley, my love.
I will never forget you, never, never.
You are my whole life
I hope you will never forget me.

[In English:]
Please come to Mexico as you promised me! We will go together to TEHUANTEPEC in August.
[Lipstick print of a kiss.]
This is specially for the back of your neck.

1939
16 February

Paris, 16 February 1939

My adorable Nick, Mi niño,
I am writing you on my bed in the American Hospital. Yesterday it was the first day I didn't have fever and they aloud me to eat a little, so I feel better. Two weeks ago I was so ill that they brought me here in an ambulance because I couldn't even walk. You know that I don't know why or how I got colibacilus on the kidneys thru the intestines, and I had such an inflammation and pains that I thought I was going to die. They took several X-rays of the kidneys and it seems that they're infected with those damn colibacilus. Now <u>I am better</u> and next Monday I will be out of this rotten hospital. I can't go to the hotel, because I would be all alone, so the wife of Marcel Duchamp invited me to stay with her for a week while I recover a little. Your telegram arrived this morning and I cried very much – of happiness, and because I miss you with all my heart and my blood. Your letter,

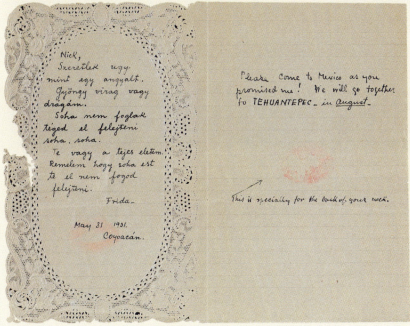

Nick,
Szeretlek ugy
mint egy anggalt.
Gyöngy virag vagy
dragám.
Soha nem foglak
téged el felejteni
soha. soha.
Te vagy a tejes életem.
Remelem hogy soha est
te el nem fogod
felejteni.
— Frida —

May 31 1931.
Coyoacán.

Please come to Mexico as you
promised me! We will go together
to TEHUANTEPEC — in August —

This is specially for the back of your neck.

31 May 1931

Paris Feb 16. 1939.

My adorable Nick. Mi niño,
I am writting you on my bed in the American Hospital. Yesterday it was the first day I didn't have fever and they aloud me to eat a little, so I feel better. Two weeks ago I was so ill that they brought me here in an ambulance because I couldn't even walk. You know that I don't know why or how I got coli-bacilus on the kidneys thru the intestines, and I had such an inflammation and pains that I thought I was going to die. They took several X rays of the kidneys and it seems that they are infected with those damn colibacilus. Now I am better and next monday I will be out of this rotten hospital. I can't go to the hotel, because I would be all alone, so the wife of Marcel Duchamp invited me to stay with her for a week while I recover a little. Your telegram arrived this morning and I cried very much — of happiness, and because I miss you with all my heart and my blood. Your letter, my sweet, came yesterday, it is so beautiful, so tender, that I have no words to tell you what a joy it gave me. I adore you my

my sweet, came yesterday, it is so beautiful, so tender, that I have no words to tell you what a joy it gave me. I adore you my love, believe me, like I never loved anyone – only Diego will be in my heart as close as you – always. I haven't tell Diego a word about all this troubles of being ill because he will worry so much, and I think in a few days I will be all right again, so it isn't worthwhile to alarm him. Don't you think so?

Besides this damn sickness I had the lousiest luck since I arrived. In first place the question of the exhibition is all a damn mess. Until I came the paintings were still in the custom house, because the s. of a b. of Breton didn't take the trouble to get them out. The photographs, which you sent <u>ages ago</u>, <u>he never received</u> – so he says – the gallery was not arranged for the exhibition <u>at all</u> and Breton has no gallery of his own *[since]* long ago. So I had to wait days and days just like an idiot till I met Marcel Duchamp (a marvellous painter) who is the only one who has his feet on the earth, among all this bunch of coocoo lunatic sons of bitches of the surrealists. He immediately got my paintings out and tried to find a gallery. Finally there was a gallery called 'Pierre Colle', which accepted the damn exhibition. Breton wants to exhibit together with my paintings 14 portraits of the XIX century (Mexicans), about 32 photographs of Alvarez Bravo, and lots of popular objects that he bought in the markets of Mexico – <u>all this junk</u>, can you beat that? For the 15 of March the gallery supose to be ready. But… the 14 oils of the XIX century must be restored and the damn restoration takes a whole month. I had to lend to Breton 200 bucks (Dlls) for the restoration because he doesn't have a penny. (I sent a cable to Diego telling him the situation and telling him that I lended to Breton that money – he was furious but now is <u>done</u> and I have nothing to do about it.) I still have money to stay here till the beginning of March, so I don't have to worry so much.

Well, after things were more or less settled as I told you, a few days ago Breton told me that the associates of Pierre Colle, an old bastard and a son of a bitch saw my paintings and found that only two were possible to be shown because the rest are too 'shocking' for the public!! I could of kill that guy and eat it afterwards, but I am so sick and tired of the whole affair that I decided to send everything to hell, and scram from this rotten Paris before I go nuts myself. You have no idea the kind of bitches these people are. They make me vomit. They are so damn 'intellectual' and rotten that I can't stand them anymore. It is really too much for my character – I rather sit on the floor in the market of Toluca and sell tortillas than have anything to do with those 'artistic' bitches of Paris.

They sit for hours in the 'cafés' warming their precious behinds, and talk without stopping about 'culture', 'art', 'Revolution' and so on and so forth thinking themselves the gods of the world, dreaming the most fantastic nonsenses, and poisoning the air with theories and theories that never come true.

[...] My ticket will last for a long time but I already have accommodations for the 'Isle de France' on the 8 of March. I hope I can take this boat. In any case I won't stay here any longer than the 15th of March. To hell with the exhibition in London. To hell with every thing concerning Breton and all this lousy place. I want to go back to you. I miss every movement of your being, your voice, your eyes, your hands, your beautiful mouth, your laugh so clear and honest. YOU. I love you my Nick. I am so happy to think I love you – to think you wait for me – you love me. My darling give many kisses to Mam[13] on my name, I never forget her. Kiss also Aria and Lea *[Nick's daughter, Arija, and ex-wife, Leja]*. For you, my heart full of tenderness and caresses. One special kiss on your neck.

Your
Xóchitl
[Written on the left side of the page:] Give my love to Mary Sklar *[Frida's friend, sister of art historian Meyer Schapiro]* if you see her and to Ruzzy *[Alex's friend, photographer Ruzzie Green]*

— 6 —

*scram from here.

My ticket will last for a long time but I already have acomodations for the "Isle de France" on the 8 of March. I hope I can take this boat. In any case I won't stay here longer than the 15th of March. ~~The~~ To hell with the exibition in London. To hell with every thing concerning Breton and all this lousy place. I want to go back to you. I miss every movement of your being, your voice, your eyes, your hands, your beautiful mouth, your laugh so clear and honest. <u>YOU</u>.

I love you my Nick. I am so happy to think I love you — to think you wait for me. You love me.

My darling give many Kisses to Mam on my name, I never forget her. Kiss also Aria and Lea. For you, my heart full of tenderness and caresses. One special kiss on your neck. Your

Xochitl

*Give my love to Mary Sklar if you see her and to Ruzzy

16 February 1939

Your words made me
feel so close to you
that I can feel near
me your eyes, your
hands, your lips.

1939
27 February

Paris, 27 February 1939

My adorable Nick,
This morning after so many days of waiting – your letter arrived. I felt so happy that before starting to read it I began to weep. My child, I really shouldn't complain about anything that happens to me in life, as long as you love me and I love you. It is so real and beautiful, that *[your letter]* makes me forget all pains and troubles, makes me forget even distance. Your words made me feel so close to you that I can feel near me your eyes, your hands, your lips. I can hear your voice and your laugh. That laugh so clean and honest that only <u>you</u> have. I'm just counting the days to go back. A month more! And we will be together again.

Darling, I made a terrible mistake. I was sure that your birthday was the 16th of <u>January</u>. If I knew it was the 16th of February I would never send that cable that caused you unhappiness and trouble. Please forgive me.

Five days ago I left the hospital, I am feeling much better and I hope I will be entirely well in a few days. I didn't go back to the damn hotel because I couldn't stay all alone. Mary Reynolds a marvellous American woman who lives with Marcel Duchamp invited me to stay at her house and I accepted gladly because she is really a nice person and doesn't have anything to do with the stinking 'artists' of the group of Breton. She is very kind to me and takes care of me wonderfully. I feel rather weak after so many days of fever because the damn infection of collibacili makes you feel rotten. The doctor tells me I must of eaten something which wasn't well cleaned (salad or raw fruits). I bet you my boots, that in Breton's house was where I got the lousy collibacili. You don't have any idea of the dirt those people live in, and the kind of food they eat. It's something incredible. I never seen anything like it before in my damn life. For a reason that I ignore, the infection went from the intestines to the bladder and the kidneys, so for 2 days I couldn't make pipi and

I felt like if I were going to explode any minute. Fortunately, everything its ok now, and the only thing I must do is to rest and to have a special diet. I am sending you here some reports from the hospital. I want you to be so sweet to give them to Mary Sklar and she will show them to Daniel Glusker *[a doctor]*, so he can have an idea of what is the matter and send me indications of what I should eat. (Tell her that for the three last days the urine tests shown that it is acid and before it was alkaline. The fever disappeared completely. I still have pain when I make pipi and a slight inflammation of the bladder, I feel tired all the time especially on the back.) Thank you, my love, for making me this favour and tell Mary that I miss her a lot and that I love her.

The question of the exhibition, finally, it's settled. Marcel Duchamp has helped me a lot and he is the only one among this rotten people who is a real guy. The show will open the <u>10th of March</u> in a gallery called 'Pierre Colle'. They say it's one of the best here. That guy Colle is the dealer of Dalí and some other big shots of the Surrealism. It will last two weeks. But I already made arrangements to take out my paintings the 23rd in order to have time to pack them and take them with me on the 25th.

[…] My darling, I must tell you, that you are a bad boy. Why did you send me that check of 400 bucks? Your friend 'Smith' is an imaginary one – very sweet indeed, but tell <u>him</u> that I will keep <u>his check untouched</u> until I come back to New York, and there we will talk things over. My Nick, you are the sweetest person I ever known. But listen darling, I don't really need that money now. I got some from Mexico, and I am a real rich bitch, you know? I have enough to stay here a month more. I have my return ticket. <u>Everything is under control</u>, so really, my love, it is not fair that you should spend anything extra. You have plenty of troubles already to cause you a new one. I have money even to go to the 'thieves market' and buy lots of junk which is one of the things I like the best. I don't have to buy dresses or stuff like that because being a 'Tehuana', I don't even wear pants nor

Paris. Feb. 27. 1939.

My adorable Nick -

This morning after so many days of waiting - your letter arrived. I felt so happy that before starting to read it I began to weep. My child, I realy shouldn't complain about any thing that happens to me in life, as long as you love me and I love you. It is so real and beautiful, that makes me forget all pains and troubles, makes me forget even distance. Your words made me feel so close to you that I can feel near me your eyes - your hands - your lips. I can hear your voice and your laugh. That laugh so clean and honest that only you have. I am just counting the days to go back. A month more! and we will be together again.

Darling, I made a terrible mistake. I was sure that your birthday was the 16th of January. If I knew it was the 16th of February I would never send that cable that caused you unhappiness and trouble. Please forgive me.

Five days ago I left the hospital, I am feeling much better and I hope I will be entirely well in a few days. I didn't go back to the damn hotel because I couldn't stay all alone. Mary Reynolds a marvelous american woman who lives with Marcel Duchamp invited me to stay at her house and I accepted gladly because she is really a nice person and doesn't have stockings either. The only things I bought here were two old-fashioned dolls, very beautiful ones. One is blond with blue eyes, the most wonderful eyes you can imagine. She is dressed as a bride. Her dress was full of dust and dirt, but I washed it, and now it looks much better. Her head is not very well-adjusted to her body because the elastic which holds it is already very old, but you and me will fix it in New York. The other one is less beautiful, but very charming. *[She]* has blond hair and very black eyes, I haven't washed her dress yet and it's dirty as hell. She only have one shoe, the other one she lost it in the market. Both are lovely, even with their heads a little bit loose. Perhaps that is which gives them so much tenderness and charm. For years I wanted to have a doll like that, because somebody broke one that I had when I was a child, and I couldn't find it again. So I am very happy having two now. I have a little bed in Mexico which will be marvellous for the bigger one. Think of two nice Hungarian names to baptize them. The two of them cost me about two dollars and a half. So you can see my darling, that my expenses are not very important. I don't have to pay hotel because Mary Reynolds doesn't allow me to go back to the hotel all by myself.

The hospital is already payed, so I don't think I will need very much money to live here. Anyway, you cannot imagine how much I appreciate your desire of helping me. I have not words to tell you what joy it gives me to think that you were willing to make me happy and to know how good hearted and adorable you are. My lover, my sweetest, mi Nick, mi vida, mi niño, te adoro.

I got thinner with the illness, so when I will be with you, you will only blow and… up she goes! the 5 floors of the La Salle Hotel. Listen kid, do you touch every day the fire 'whatchamacallit' which hangs on the corridor of our staircase? Don't forget to do it every day. Don't forget either to sleep on your tiny little cushion, because I love it. Don't kiss anybody else while reading the signs and names on the streets. Don't take anybody else for a ride to our Central Park. It belongs only to Nick and Xóchitl.

Don't kiss anybody on the couch of your office. Only Blanche Heys *[Nick's friend]* can give you a massage on your neck. You can only kiss as much as you want, Mam. Don't make love with anybody, if you can help it. Only if you find a real F.W. but <u>don't love her</u>.

Play with your electric train once in a while if you don't come home very tired. How is Joe Jinks *[a comic-strip character]*? How is the man who massages you twice a week? I hate him a little, because he took you away from me many hours. Have you fenced a lot? How is Georgio?

Why do you say that your trip to Hollywood was only half successful? Tell me all about it. My darling, don't work so hard if you can help it. Because you get tired on your neck and on your back. Tell Mam to take care of yourself, and to make you rest when you feel tired. Tell her that I am much more in love with you, that you are my darling and my lover, and that while I am away she must love you more than ever to make you happy.

Does your neck bother you very much? I am sending you here millions of kisses for your beautiful neck to make it feel better. All my tenderness and all my caresses to your body, from your head to your feet. Every inch of it I kiss from the distance.
[Lipstick print at the bottom of the page.]

Play very often Maxine Sullivan's disc on the gramophone. I will be there with you listening to her voice. I can see you lying on the blue couch, with your white cape, I see you shooting at the sculpture near the fireplace. I see clearly, the spring jumping on the air, and I can hear your laugh – just like a child's laugh, when you got it right. Oh my darling Nick, I adore you so much. I need you so, that my heart hurts.

I imagine Blanche will be here the first week of March. I will be so happy to see her because she is a real person, sweet and sincere, and she is to me like a part of yourself. How are Aria and Lea? Please give my love to them. Also give my love to the kid Ruzzie, tell him that he is a swell guy.

My darling, do you need anything from Paris? Please tell me, I will be so happy to get you any thing you may need.

If Eugenia phones you, please tell her that I lost her dress and that is why I didn't write. How is that wench?

If you see Rosemary give her lots of kisses, she is ok. To Mary Sklar, lots of love. I miss her very much.

To you, my loveliest Nick, all my heart, blood and all my being. I adore you.
Frida.
[Lipstick print at the bottom of the page.] [Written sideways in margin:] The photographs you sent finally arrived.

1939
13 June

13 June 1939

Nick darling,
I got my wonderful picture you send to me, I find it even more beautiful than in New York. Diego says that it is as marvellous as a Piero della Francesca. To me is more than that, it is a treasure, and besides, it will always remind me *[of]* that morning we had breakfast together in the Barbizon Plaza Drug Store, and afterwards we went to your shop to take photos. This one was one of them. And now I have it near me. You will always be inside the magenta rebozo (on the left side). Thanks million times for sending it.

When I received your letter, few days ago, I didn't know what to do. I must tell you that I couldn't help weeping. I felt that

13 June 1939

#3-

a trouble in your life in any case.

Please forgive me for acting just like an old fashion sweet heart asking you to give me back my letters, it is ridiculous on my part, but I do it for you, not for me, because I imagine that you don't have any interest in having those papers with you.

While I was writting this letter Rose telephoned and told me that you got married already. I have nothing to say about what I felt.
I hope you will be happy, very happy.
If you find time once in a while, please write to me just a few words telling me how you are, will you do it?
Give my love to Mam and to Ruwzy.
I imagine you must be very bussy now and will not have time to get for me the date when Dorothy Hale killed herself, please be so sweet to ask Mam to make for me that favor, I can't send the picture till I know that damn date. And it is urgent that this wench of Claire Luce has the painting in order to get from her the bucks.
Another thing, if you write to Blanche Hays, tell her that I send all my love to her. The same, and very specially, to the Sklars.
Thanks for the magnificent photo, again and again. Thanks for your last letter, and for all the treasures you gave me.

Love

Frida

Please forgive me for having phoned to you that evening. I won't do it any more.

13 June 1939

something was in my throat, just as if I had swallowed the whole world. I don't know yet if I was sad, jealous or angry, but the sensation I felt was in first place of a great despair. I have read your letter many times, too many, I think, and now I realize things that I couldn't see at first. Now, I understand everything perfectly clearly, and the only thing I want, is to tell you with my best words, that you deserve in life the best, the very best, because you are one of the few people in this lousy world who are honest to themselves, and that is the only thing that really counts. I don't know why I could feel hurt 1 minute because you are happy. It is so silly the way Mexican wenches (like myself) see life sometimes! But you know that, and I'm sure you will forgive me for behaving so stupidly. Nevertheless you have to understand that no matter what happens to us in life, you will always be, for myself, the same Nick I met one morning in New York in 18th E. 48th St.

I told Diego that you were going to marry soon. he said that to Rose and Miguel, the other day when they came to visit us, so I had to tell them that it was true. I am terribly sorry to have said it before asking you if it was ok, but now it's done, and I beg you to forgive my indiscretion.

I want to ask from you a great favour, please, send by mail the little cushion, I don't want anybody else to have it. I promise to make another one for you, but I want that one you have now on the couch downstairs, near the window. Another favour: Don't let 'her' touch the fire signals on the stairs (you know which ones). If you can, and if it isn't too much trouble, don't go to Coney Island, especially to the <u>Half Moon</u>, with her. Take down the photo of myself which was on the fireplace, and put it in Mam's room in the shop, I'm sure she still likes me as much as she did before. Besides, it is not so nice for the other lady to see my portrait in your house. I wish I could tell you many many things but I think it is no use to bother you. I hope you will understand without words all my wishes.

Darling, are you sure it is not too much bother for you to arrange for me the question of the painting of Mrs Luce *[publisher of Vanity Fair and friend of Dorothy Hale]*? Everything is ready to send it, but I wish you could get for me only one detail that I need very badly. I don't remember <u>the date</u> when Dorothy Hale committed suicide, and it is necessary to write it down on the painting, so if you could find out, by phone, somewhere, I would be very happy. Not to bother you so much, please write down in a piece of paper the exact date and mail it to me. About the painting, you just leave it in your office (it is a small one) and as soon as you think that Mrs Luce is in New York, just call her up and let her know that the damn picture is there. She will send for it I am sure.

About my letters to you, if they are on the way, just give them to Mam and she will mail them back to me. I don't want to be a trouble in your life in any case. Please forgive me for acting just like an old-fashioned sweetheart asking you to give me back my letters, it is ridiculous on my part, but I do it for you, not for me, because I imagine that you don't have any interest in having those papers with you.

While I was writing this letter Rose telephoned and told me that you got married already. I have nothing to say about what I felt. I hope you will be happy, very happy.

If you find time once in a while, please write to me just a few words telling me how you are, will you do it?

Give my love to Mam and to Ruzzy.

I imagine you must be very busy now and will not have time to get the date when Dorothy Hale killed herself, please be so sweet to ask Mam to make for me that favour, I can't send the picture till I know the damn date. And it is urgent that this wench of Claire Luce has the painting in order to get from her the bucks.

Frida with Magenta Rebozo, 1939

Thanks Nickolasito for all your kindness, for the dreams about me, for your sweet thoughts, for everything.

Another thing, if you write to Blanche Heys, tell her that I send all my love to her. The same, and very specially, to the Sklars.

Thanks for the magnificent photo, again and again. Thanks for your last letter, and for all the treasures you gave me.
Love,
Frida

[Handwritten in pencil at the bottom of the page:] Please forgive me for having phoned you that evening. I won't do it anymore.

1939
13 October

Coyoacán, 13 October 1939

Nick darling,
I couldn't write to you before, since you left, my situation with Diego was worse and worse, till came to an end. Two weeks ago we began the divorce. I have no words to tell you how much I been suffering and knowing how much I love Diego you must understand that these troubles will never end in my life, but after the last fight I had with him (by phone) because it is almost a month that I don't see him, I understood that for him it is much better to leave me. He told me the worst things you can imagine and the dirtiest insults I ever expected from him. I can't tell you here all the details because it is impossible, but one day, when you will be in Mexico, I can explain to you the whole thing. Now I feel so rotten and lonely that it seems to me that nobody in the world has suffer the way I do, but of course it will be different, I hope, in a few months.

Darling, I must tell you that I am not sending the painting with Miguel. Last week I had to sell it to somebody thru Misrachi because I needed the money to see a lawyer. Since I came back from New York I don't accept a damn cent from Diego, the reasons you must understand. I will never accept money from any man till I die. I want to beg you to forgive me for doing that with a painting that was done for you. But I will keep my promise and paint another one as soon as I feel better. It is a cinch.

I haven't seen the Covarrubias so the photos you sent to them are still with me. I love all the photographs you were so sweet to send, they are really swell. Thanks a lot for them. I send Diego your check. Has he thank you for it? He didn't see the photos because I don't think he will be very much interested in seeing my face near his. So I kept them all for me.

Listen baby, please don't think badly about me because I haven't seen Juan O'Gorman about your house. It is only because I don't want to see anybody that is near Diego, and I hope you will understand. Please write to Juan directly. His address is: Calle Jardín No. 10, Villa Obregón, D.F. México. I am sure he will be very happy in doing what you wish.

I am so glad to hear that Arija is well and will be with you soon. I think you will bring her along to Mexico next time, won't you? I am sure she will enjoy it very much.

How about your own troubles? It is all set with the girl? In your last letter you sound happier and less preocupated, and I am glad as hell for that. Have you heard from Mary Sklar? Whenever you see her tell her that inspite my negligence to write I do love her just the same as ever.

Tell Mam that I will send with Miguel the presents I promised her, and thank her for the sweet letter she sent me. Tell her that I love her with all my heart.

Thanks Nickolasito for all your kindness, for the dreams about me, for your sweet thoughts, for everything. Please forgive me for not writing as soon as I received your letters, but let me tell

Coyoacán, 13 de Octubre de 1939.

Nick darling,

      I couldn't write to you before, since you left, my situation with Diego was worst and worst, till came to and end. Two weeks ago we began the divorce. I have no words to tell you how much I been suffering and knowing how much I love Diego you must understand that this troubles will never end in my life, but after the last fight I had with him (by phone) because it is almost a month that I don't see him, I understood that for him it is much better xxxxxxxxxxxxxxxxxxxxx to leave me. He told me the worst things you can imagine and the dirtiest insults I ever expected from him. I can8t tell you here all the details because it is imposible, but one day, when you will be in Mexico, I can explain to you the whole thing. Now I feel so rotten and lonely that it seems to me that nobody in the world has suffer the way I do, but ofcourse it will be different I hope, in a few months.

      Darling, I must tell you that I am not sending the painting with Miguel. Last week I had to sell it to somebody thru Misrachi because I needed the money to see a lawyer. Since I came bakk from New York I don't accept a damn cent from Diego, the reasons you must understand. I will never accept money from any man till I die. I want to beg you to forgive me for doing that with a painting that was done for you. But I will keep my promise and paint another one as soon as I feel better. It is a cinch.

      I haven4t seen the Covarrubias, so the photos you sent to them are still with me. I love all the photographs you were so sweet to send, they are realy xxxxx swell. Thanks a lot for them. I send Diego your chek. Has he thank you for it? He didn't see the photos because I dont think he will be very much interested in seeing my face near his. So I kept them all for me.

      Listen baby, please dont think badly about me because I haven't seen Juan O'Gorman about your house. It is only because I dont want to see anybody that is near Diego, and I hope you will understand. Please write to Juan directly. His adress is: Calle Jardin No. 10 Villa Obregón D.F. México. I am sure he will be very happy in doing what you wish.

      I am so glad to hear that Arija is well and will be with you soon. I think you will bring her along to Mexico nex time, wont you? I am sure she will enjoy it very much.

      How about your own troubles? It is all set with the girl? In your last letter you sound happier and less preocupated, and I am glad as hell for that. Have you heard from Mary Sklar? When ever you see her tell her that inspite my negligence to write I do love her just the same as ever.

      Tell Mam that I will send with Miguel the presents I promised her, and thank her for the sweet letter she sent me. Tell her that I love her with all my heart.

      Thanks Nickolasito for all your kindness, for the dreams about me, for your sweet thoughts, for every thing. Please forgive me for not writting as soon as I received your letters, but let me tell you kid, that this time has been the worst in my whole life and I am surprised that one can live thru it.

      My sister and the babies send their love to you.

      Dont forget me and be good boy. I love you,

                            Frida

13 October 1939

Coyoacán. December 18. 1939.

Nick darling.

You will say that I am a complete bastard and a s. of a b.! I asked you money and didn't even thank you for it! That is realy the limit kid! Please forgive me. I was sick two weeks. My foot again and grippe. Now I thank you a million times for your kind favor and about the paying back I want you to be so sweet to wait till January. The Arensberg from Los Angeles will buy a picture. I am sure I will have the bucks next year and immediately I will send you back your hundred bucks. It is ok with you? In case you need them before I could arrange something else. In any case I want to tell you that it was realy sweet of you to lend me that money. I needed it so much ——

I had to give up the idea of renting my house to tourists, be-

18 December 1939

you kid, that this time has been the worst in my whole life and I am surprised that one can live thru it.

My sister and the babies send their love to you.

Don't forget me and be a good boy. I love you,
Frida

1939
18 December

Coyoacán, 18 December 1939

Nick darling,
You will say that I am a complete bastard and a s. of a b.! I asked you money and didn't even thank you for it! That is really the limit kid! Please forgive me. I was sick two weeks. My foot again and grippe. Now I thank you a million times for your kind favour, and about the paying back I want you to be so sweet to wait till January. The Arensberg from Los Angeles will buy a picture. I am sure I will have the bucks next year and immediately I will send you back your hundred bucks. It is ok with you? In case you need them before I could arrange something else. In any case I want to tell you that it was really sweet of you to lend me that money. I needed it so much.

I had to give up the idea of renting my house to tourists, because to fix the house would cost a lot of money, which I didn't have and Misrachi didn't lend me, and in second place because my sister wasn't exactly the person indicated to run such a business. She doesn't speak a damn word of English and would of been impossible for her to get along well. So now I am hoping only in my own work. I been working quite a lot. In January I will send to Julien two or three things. I will expose four paintings in the surrealist show, which Paalen will have in Inés Amor Gallery… little by little I'll be able to solve my problems and survive!!

How is your sinus? How long were you in the hospital and how it worked? Tell me some things about yourself. Your last letter was only about myself but not a word about how you feel, your work, your plans, etc. I received a letter from Mary. She told me the magnificent news that she will have a baby. I am more than happy about it, because Sol and herself will be just crazy of joy with a kid.

Tell me about Mam. Kiss her one hundred times for me. Beginning in her eyes and finishing wherever is more convenient for both. Also kiss Ruzzy in the cheek. What is Miguelito and Rose doing? Are you coming with them to Mexico? I imagine you have already some other plans because you don't say a damn word about it in your letters. Is there another wench in your life? What nationality?

Give my love to Lea and to your baby. Were they happy in France? Kid, don't forget about me. Write once in a while. If you don't have very much time take a piece of toilet paper and in… those moments… write your name in it. That will be enough to know that you still remember this wench!

All my love to you.
Frida

1940 January

January 1940

Nick darling,
I received the hundred bucks of this month, I don't know how to thank you. I couldn't write before because I had an infeccion in the hand which didn't let me work or write or anything. Now I am better and am working like hell. I have to finish a big painting and start small things to send to Julien this month.

its the best of all. The other wenches are OK too but the one of myself is a real F.W. (Do you still remember the translation? — "forking wonder")
I think Julien will sell for me this month or next (sic) a painting to the Arensberg. (Los Angeles) If he does, I told him to pay back to you the money you already send me — because it is easier to pay little by little than to wait till the end of the year. Don't you think so? You can't have any idea of the strange feeling I have owing you money. I wish you would understand. How is Arija? and Lea? Please tell me things of yourself!!! Are you better of your sinus trouble? I feel lousy. Every day worse and worse. Any way I am working — But event that I don't know how and why? Do you know who came to Mexico? That awful wench of Ione Robinson. I imagine she thinks that the road is clear now...... I don't see any body. I am almost all day in my house. Diego came the other day to try to convince me that nobody in the world is like me! Lots of crap kid! I cant forgive him — And that is all. —
My love to Mam.
Your mexican wench
Frida.

How is this new year for you? How is Jue Shup? How is New York? How is Ella Bella? And the woman who you skated?

January 1940

January 1940

6 February 1940

The 17th it will be a show of surrealist painting and everybody in Mexico has become a surrealist because all are going to take part in it. This world is completely cockeyed, kid!!

Mary wrote to me and sayed that she hasn't seen you for a long time. What are you doing? It seems to me that you treat me now only as a friend you are helping, but nothing more. You never tell me about yourself, and not even about your work. I saw 'Coronet' and my photo its the best of all. The other wenches are ok too but the one of myself – is a real F.W. (Do you still remember the translation? 'fucking wonder')

I think Julien will sell for me this month or next a painting to the Arensberg (Los Angeles) *[art collector and critic]*. If he does, I told him to pay back to you the money you already send me because it is easier to pay little by little than to wait till the end of the year – don't you think so? You can't have any idea of the strange feeling I have owing you money. I wish you would understand. How is Arija? And Lea? Please tell me things of yourself!!! Are you better of your sinus trouble?

I feel lousy. Every day worse and worse. Anyway I am working but even that I don't know how and why? Do you know who came to Mexico? That awful wench of Ione Robinson. I imagine she thinks that the road is clear now!... I don't see anybody. I am almost all day in my house. Diego came the other day to try to convince me that nobody in the world is like me! Lots of crap kid. I can't forgive him – and that is all –

My love to Mam.
Your Mexican wench
Frida

[Written sideways in left margin:] How is this new year for you? How is Joe Jinks? How is New York? How is the La Salle? And the woman you always shooted?

1940
6 February

Coyoacán, 6 February 1940

Nick darling,

I got the bucks, thanks again for your kindness. Miguel will take one big painting for the show in the Modern Museum. The other big one I will send to Julien. He proposed me to have a show next November so I am working hard. Besides I applied for the Guggenheim, and Carlos Chavez *[Mexican composer]* is helping me on that, if it works I can go to New York in October–November for my show. I haven't send small paintings to Julien because it's better to send three or four than one by one.

What about you? Not a single word I know about what the hell are you doing. I imagine all your plans about Mexico were given up. Why? Do you have another wench? A swell one? Please kid tell me something. At least tell me how happy you are or what on earth are you thinking to do this year or next.

How is little Mam? Give her my love.

I have to give you a bad news: I cut my hair, and look just like a ferry. Well, it will grow again, I hope!

How is Arija? And Lea? Have you seen Mary and Sol?

Write to me, please, one evening instead of reading Joe Jinks remember that I exist on this planet.

Yours
Frida

Feb. 6. 1940.
Coyoacán.

Nick darling.

I got the bucks – thanks again for your kindness – Miguel will take one big painting for the show on the Modern Museum. The other big one I will send to Julien. He proposed me to have a show next november so I am working hard. Besides I applied for the Guggenheim, and Carlos Chavez is helping me on that, if it works I can go to new York in October – november for my show. I haven't send small paintings to Julien because its better to send three or four than one by one.

What about you? not a single

LETTER TO:

Georgia O'Keeffe

A Profound Understanding

I thought of you a lot and never forget your wonderful hands and the colour of your eyes.

Georgia O'Keeffe next to her painting *Horse's Skull with White Rose*, 1931

Georgia O'Keeffe (1887–1986) and Frida met in New York in December 1931, at the opening of Diego's solo exhibition at the Museum of Modern Art. Diego later bragged that his wife had flirted with O'Keeffe.[14] (Diego delighted in Frida's involvements with women but became jealous and angry when he learned of her affairs with men.) Georgia was 20 years older than Frida and already a recognized artist for her paintings of New York skyscrapers, details of flowers and Southwest landscapes. Nonetheless the women had much in common: both were in complicated marriages with older men who were prominent in the art world, and both grappled with being taken seriously as women artists.

Frida wrote the letter transcribed here from Detroit upon hearing that her friend was in hospital. Georgia had been struggling with her mental health, a struggle exacerbated by her husband's infidelity, and was hospitalized for two months. A few weeks after writing, when Frida arrived in New York, she visited Georgia and in a letter to Clifford Wight, one of Rivera's assistants, she later wrote: 'She didn't make love to me that time, I think on account of her weakness. Too bad.'[15]

Frida and Georgia are known to have met on a few other occasions, including in New York on the opening night of Frida's first solo exhibition at the Julien Levy Gallery in November 1938, and then in Mexico in 1951, when Georgia visited Frida while travelling. Frida took inspiration from Georgia; this is particularly evident in her portrayals of plant life, such as the 1945 painting *Magnolias*. Georgia had a pioneering role in American Modernism and was the first woman to have a retrospective at the Museum of Modern Art in New York (1946). Frida Kahlo and Georgia O'Keeffe would go on to become two of the most celebrated female artists of the twentieth century.

March the first – 1933.

Georgia,

Was wonderful to hear your voice again. Every day since I called you and many times before, months ago I wanted to write you a letter. I wrote many, but every one seemed more stupid and empty and I torn them up. I can't write in English all I would like to tell, especially to you. I am sending this one because I promised it to you. I felt terrible when Sibil Brown told me that you were sick but I still don't know what is the matter with you. Please Georgia dear if you can't write, ask Stieglietz to do it for you and let me know how are you feeling Will you? I'll be in Detroit two more weeks.

I would like to tell you

1933
1 March

March the first 1933

Georgia,
Was wonderful to hear your voice again. Every day since I called you and many times before, months ago I wanted to write you a letter. I wrote many, but every one seemed more stupid and empty and I torn them up. I can't write in English all I would like to tell, especially to you. I am sending this one because I promised it to you. I felt terrible when Sibil Brown told me that you were sick but I still don't know what is the matter with you. Please Georgia dear if you can't write, ask Stieglietz *[photographer and O'Keeffe's husband]* to do it for you and let me know how are you feeling will you? I'll be in Detroit two more weeks.

I would like to tell you everything that happened to me since the last time we saw each other, but most of them are sad and you mustn't know sad things now. After all I shouldn't complain because I have been happy in many ways though. Diego is good to me, and you can't imagine how happy he has been working on the frescoes here. I have been painting a little too and that helped. I thought of you a lot and never forget your wonderful hands and the colour of your eyes. I will see you soon. I am sure that in New York I will be much happier. If you still in the hospital when I come back I will bring you flowers, but it is so difficult to find the ones I would like for you. I would be so happy if you could write me even two words. I like you very much Georgia.

Frieda

[Written in the left margin:] My address here: The Wardel Apts. 15 Kirby, Detroit

LETTERS TO:

Ignacio Aguirre

A Passionate Affair

Write to me — I'll await your letter as if you yourself were coming to me.

Ignacio Aguirre in front of a work by Bernard Silberstein (1905–1999), Mexico City, 1940

Ignacio Aguirre (1900–1990), a Mexican painter and printmaker, had a passionate but short-lived affair with Frida in 1935 that lasted around three months. After discovering that her husband was having an affair with her sister, and realizing that he was never going to be faithful to her, Frida started having serious love affairs of her own, although, unlike Diego, she was discreet about her liaisons, to avoid her husband's anger. It was during this time that she connected with Nacho, as she called him. Frida and Ignacio met at his home or in other rendezvous spots.

Originally from Jalisco state, Ignacio fought in the Mexican Revolution (1910–20) alongside the Constitutionalists who desired a democratic government, and then later in support of Álvaro Obregón. In the years immediately following the Revolution, he participated in the government's Misiones Culturales (Cultural Missions), which aimed to make education, art and culture available to the whole country, and he travelled to rural areas of Mexico to paint murals in schools and other public buildings. In the late 1930s, he joined the Taller de Gráfica Popular (People's Graphic Workshop), an artist's print collective in Mexico City that was concerned with making art to advance social causes. Ignacio's work often depicted rural life, indigenous communities and revolutionary themes.

When their romance came to an end, Ignacio kept Frida's letters and photos in a small lacquered box made of aromatic wood from Olinalá, in the state of Guerrero, and inscribed with his name. The box may have been a gift from Frida: she had many such boxes in her home. In 1986, Ignacio gave a lecture about Frida, and it is evident that he retained many fond memories of her: 'Frida is the event of each day, with birds and flowers, forget-me-nots, pelicans, marigolds, the moisture of the garden, and the aroma of a burning comal.... Scandalously beautiful Frida.'[16]

1935
19 August

19 August 1935

I kept your letter like a treasure – your voice gave me the purest joy, I didn't know what to do and I began to write this letter, which will be unable to tell you, with my words, everything I would like to say – everything you deserve for giving me so much! – your beauty – your hands – you. I wish I could be so pretty for you! I wish I could give you everything that you've never had, and even so you wouldn't know how wonderful it is to be able to love you. I will wait all the minutes until I can see you. Wait for me at a quarter past six on Wednesday – below, in the big hallway of your house, because I think that's easiest –

Call me tomorrow at six in the afternoon; I just want to hear your voice, even if only for a moment. If you call me, I will gather many little flowers for you and I will bring them to you on Wednesday, but if you don't call me, I'll bring them to you anyway – so many that they could make a garden on your chest – the colour of humid earth. The frogs are still singing for us – and our river is waiting – the chaste town is looking at the Great Bear constellation – and as for me – I adore you.

1935
24 August

24 August 1935

Call me any morning after ten o'clock – I want to see you – if we're unable to arrange where to meet by phone, write to me at 'Poste Restante' Coyoacán. In any case, write to me – I'll await your letter as if you yourself were coming to me.

→
Frida Kahlo, *Self Portrait with Curly Hair*, 1935, oil on canvas, 19.3 × 14.7 cm

Your eyes
Your marvellous hands – fine as antennae – you. Have been close to me these days.

IGNACIO AGUIRRE

[Acrostic for Ignacio:]

Imán (Magnet)
Gaviota (Seagull)
Niño (Child)
Amor (Love)
Canela (Cinnamon)
Isla (Island)
Océano (Ocean)

Don't laugh at me for writing these words with the letters of your name.

I know that no word can express who you are – but let me think – believe – that you can feel how much I care for you.

1935
12 September

12 September 1935

Why didn't you call me this morning? I tried to locate you at all the numbers I could think of – Aviation – your house on Liverpool – M's – and nothing. I was very sad and worried. Are you still ill? I'm hoping you'll call this afternoon, but you can't imagine what I would have given today – this morning – to hear your voice.

What you were thinking yesterday is a lie! You don't know how I care for you, how I need you. Believe it. Will you? I adore you.

[Drawing of a flower with antennae.] Antennae of my life
I slept with your flower.
It is now twelve… you're not going to call me?
I want to see you – to be with you close close
You left me flowers on my shoulder – red flowers

Nacho – Nachito
[Acrostic for Nacho:]
Niño (Child)
Amor (Love)
Centro (Centre)
Hombre (Man)
Onda (Wave)

1935
14 October

14 October 1935

[Telegram.]
Nachito: they won't let us in *[to see Ignacio, who was ill]*. Get better soon. I miss you a lot. I'll write to you later. Write to me at Londres 127, Coyoacán. Frieda

1935
20 October

20 October 1935

Nachito my love, I arrived well. I'm writing to you from M's house 10 minutes after seeing you. I'm sorry to feel nervous around you. But you can understand that, can't you? I care for you more and more every moment and I wish I could see you for more hours – more hours that are really ours without time or anything stolen from life – tonight when you read this letter, I hope that you'll be with me – that you'll see me – your eyes, Nacho, are two black birds that caress me – I want you to see the marvellous colour of your body and for you to feel why it amazes me with the greatest joy – to be loved – I ask you – for the first time – do it with all the affection, yours and mine together – love
Call me tomorrow

I wish I could give you everything that you've never had, and even so you wouldn't know how wonderful it is to be able to love you.

Undated

Nachito,

I'm very sorry for what happened involving a friend of yours, and believe me that in no way did I do it thinking that it might upset you. I consider you so different from that man that I am completely sure that you will understand my attitude in an intelligent way. If what I did offended you in the slightest, I beg you to try to understand a passion, why I did it and I would sincerely beg you to forgive the violent way in which I reacted against a person that you consider a friend, but at the same time, when it comes to him, I don't regret for a moment having been the one who put the price on such a coward. I hope you understand what I'm telling you as I would like, but above all I ask you to be honest with me and tell me what you think about the matter, if you think that I was not right I will know how to understand, and the only thing that worries and interests me now is that it not be an incident of this kind that could change something between us that would be irreparable – you know what.

Please call me as soon as you can – I'll be in all morning tomorrow.

LETTER TO:

Jacqueline Lamba

A Close Tie

I will continue writing to you with my eyes, always.

Jacqueline Lamba and Frida, Mexico, 1938

F rench artist Jacqueline Lamba (1910–1993) travelled to Mexico in 1938 with her husband André Breton on a cultural commission and with the intention of meeting Leon Trotsky who, having been granted political asylum by the Mexican government, was staying at Frida's family home with his wife. Frida and Diego also offered hospitality to Breton and Lamba. The three couples spent a lot of time together and travelled around the Mexican countryside. Frida and Jacqueline got along well and became close.

When Frida went to Paris in 1939, she initially stayed with the Bretons. Their home was small and cramped, and Frida shared a room with the couple's daughter, Aube, so she did not stay for long. At a market in Paris, Frida acquired two second-hand dolls; one of them appears in Frida's 1943 painting *The Bride Frightened at Seeing Life Opened* (see p. 137), which shows a blonde doll in a white dress looking at a selection of ripe, luscious fruit. Jacqueline and her daughter stayed with Frida for several months in the early 1940s while the Frenchwoman considered leaving Breton.[17] The bride doll in the painting may represent Jacqueline contemplating what life holds for her outside her marriage.

Jacqueline painted in different styles throughout her life, embracing Surrealism during her marriage to Breton, while later painting Expressionist landscapes during her second marriage to sculptor David Hare. In the last few decades of her life, her art became more abstract and lyrical, exploring themes of nature, light and fluidity. Jacqueline's first solo exhibition was held at the Norlyst Gallery in New York in April 1944, but her work went unappreciated for many years. In 2023, the Weinstein Gallery in San Francisco held a retrospective exhibition featuring pieces from different periods of her life.

Frida wrote this draft of a letter in her diary. Although there is no name or date, it is believed to be to Jacqueline.

Undated diary entries

←

Frida Kahlo, *The Bride Frightened at Seeing Life Opened*, 1943, oil on canvas, 63 × 81.5 cm

Letter:
Since you wrote to me, on that clear and distant day, I have wanted to explain to you that I can't leave the days, or return in time to another time. I haven't forgotten you – the nights are long and difficult.

The water. The ship and the dock and the departure that had you looking so small from my eyes, imprisoned in that round porthole that you were watching to keep me in your heart. All of this is intact. Then came the days, news of you. Today I wish that the sun should touch you. I tell you that your girl is my girl, the puppet characters arranged in their large glass room belong to both of us.

Yours is the huipil with the magenta ribbons. Mine are the old plazas of your Paris, above all of them, the marvellous Des Vosges, so forgotten and so firm. The snails and the bride-doll is yours also – that's to say, she is you. Her dress is the same one that she didn't want to take off on the day of the wedding to no one, when we found her almost asleep on the dirty sidewalk of some street.

My skirts with the lace ruffles, and the old blouse that she always wore make the portrait absent, of just one person. But the colour of your skin, your eyes, and your hair change with the wind of Mexico. The death of the old man pained us so much that we called and were together.

You also know that everything that my eyes see and that I touch with myself, from all distances, is Diego. The caress of the fabric, the colour of colour, the wires, the nerves, the pencils, the pages, the powder, the cells, the war and the sun, everything that is lived in the minutes of the not-clocks and not-calendars and the empty not-looks, are him. You felt it, that's why you let the ship take you from Le Havre where you never said goodbye to me.

I will continue writing to you with my eyes, always. Kiss *[Word crossed out:]* the girl *[Written in a different pen:]* Aub

JACQUELINE LAMBA

LETTERS TO:

Josep Bartolí

A Visceral Connection

I will invent new words to tell you in all of them that I love you like no one else.

Josep Bartolí and Frida

Josep Bartolí (1910–1995) was a Catalan artist who lived in Mexico and the United States in the mid-1940s. He probably met Frida earlier, but they connected in June 1946 when she was in New York for spinal surgery. Her sister Cristina brought him to see Frida at the hospital. When Frida returned to Mexico, they maintained a correspondence, and Bartolí, as Frida always called him, visited her in August of that same year. Frida signed her letters to him 'Mara', the nickname Bartolí gave her, short for *maravillosa* (marvellous), so that if her letters were intercepted, their affair would remain secret.

Born in Barcelona, Bartolí had worked as a newspaper illustrator and was active in trade unions and left-wing politics. He fought in the Spanish Civil War (1936–39) and fled to France in 1939 when the Spanish Republic fell to Franco. Along with thousands of other Spanish refugees, he was incarcerated in internment camps in France. He drew scenes of his time in the camps with charcoal in a notebook that he kept hidden in the sand. Fleeing to Mexico in 1943, he published his book of drawings, *Campos de Concentración 1939–1943* (*Concentration Camps 1939–1943*), which showed the brutal reality of life in the camps. In 1945, he moved to the United States and joined the staff of *Holiday* magazine.

Bartolí and Frida's affair lasted about three years. It was for the most part a long-distance relationship as her health was in decline and she was unable to travel. Bartolí cherished and kept his private communications from Frida until his death in 1995.[18]

1946
29 August

29 August 1946

Bartolí, last night I felt as if many wings were caressing me all over, as if there were mouths on the tips of your fingers that were kissing my skin.

The atoms of my body are yours and they vibrate together to love us. I want to live and be strong to love you with all the tenderness that you deserve, to give you everything that is good in me, and to make you feel that you are not alone. Near or far, I want you to feel accompanied by me, to live intensely with me, but without my love hindering you in any way in your work or in your plans, for me to be such an intimate part of your life, for me to be yourself. That if I take care of you, it will never be by demanding anything from you, but rather by letting you live freely, because in all your actions, you will have my complete approval. I love you as you are, I love your voice, everything you say, what you do, what you project. I feel like I have always loved you, since you were born, and before, when you were conceived. And sometimes I feel like you were born to me. I would like all things and people to care for you and love you and be proud, like me, to have you. You are so fine and so good that you don't deserve for me to hurt your life.

I would write to you for hours and hours, I will learn stories to tell you, I will invent new words to tell you in all of them that I love you like no one else.

Mara.

August 29 Our first afternoon alone

←
Frida Kahlo, *Tree of Hope, Stand Fast*, 1946, oil on masonite, 55.9 × 40.6 cm

1946
20 October

20 October 1946

My Bartolí-Jose-Giuseppe-my red one, I don't know how to write love letters. But I wanted to tell you that my whole being opened for you. Since I fell in love with you everything is transformed and is full of beauty. I would like to give you the prettiest colours, I want to kiss you... I want our dream worlds to be one. I would like to see from your eyes, hear from your ears, feel with your skin, and kiss with your mouth. In order to see you from below... I would like to be the shadow that is born from the soles of your feet and that lengthens along the ground upon which you walk.... I want to be the water that bathes you, the light that gives you form, I wish that my substance were your substance, that your voice should come out of my throat so as to caress me from inside.... In your desire and in your revolutionary struggle to make a better human life for everyone, I want to accompany you and help you, loving you, and in your laughter find my joy. If sometimes you suffer, I want to fill you with tenderness so that you feel better. When you need me, you will always find me near you, waiting for you always. And I would like to be light and subtle when you want to be alone.

It was the thirst of many years contained in our body.... Forgive me if all these things that I write may seem stupidities to you, but I believe that in love there is neither intelligence nor stupidity. Love is like an aroma, like a current, like rain. You know, my sky, you rain on me and I, like the earth, receive you.

Mara

Love is like an aroma, like a current, like rain. You know, my sky, you rain on me and I, like the earth, receive you.

1946
November

November 1946

Say hello to Ella and Boit and Silvia. I'm going to tell Anita to bring Enrique's wife around. I really want to meet her.

Three kittens were born at the house, to a little black cat – they are wonderful.
You'll see them when you come.

What colour petticoat should I make for when you return? DON'T FORGET TO TELL ME.

I love our little house in N.Y. and since your drawing arrived – I look at it every day, and I live every moment with you since I cannot go to all the places that you go, I will wait for you every day – in the armchair or in bed. Keep me always in your heart. I will never forget you.

Your Mara
who adores you

[In the right margin:] My next letter will be less idiotic, I promise.

1946
6 December

6 December 1946

[...] You are my life, my air, my sky, my flowers, my living world, my dreams, the little objects that I love, my hands (doves for you), my eyes. I want you to love me always. I don't know how we will resolve things. I don't know, but I feel that you are going to take me with you – inside of your being, wherever, whenever you want to go, that you will open the doors of life for me, and give me all the tenderness that I need so much.... Now nothing means anything without you.... Don't forget me.

1947
October

October 1947

[...] Please tell me what plans you have.
What will you do after San Fco?
Will you go to Brazil? May I go with you?
Will you come to Mexico? Will you let me see you?
Will you go to New York, will you wait for me?
I need to see you!
I love you, my child, my Bartolí, my tree of hope. My Mexican sky, my life.
Yes, I have drawn a bit, I paint. And nothing more.
I rarely go out, I can read, sew, and I've even learned to cook a bit. And, above all, it is you that guides my life.

I care for our plant. The grey kitten died. I now have doves, there are three that nested and the first babies that they have, you will meet. Alright?

I adore you – I live you – I sky you – I care for you.
Mara

[In the left margin:] I'm in love with you.
[In the right margin:] I hear your voice… I hear it every day.

Undated

Please don't ever tell me again that my doves forget you. They are so much yours that nothing can make you be far from them. You love them, and they feel close to you in the safest nest of their lives. No hunter would dare to even look at them. With your love, you give them the treasure they've always searched for.

Sweetheart of my life, tell me something about your work, about the plans you've made with Enrique, about the perspectives you seek to achieve what you want to do there, on the other side of

Frida Kahlo, self-portrait for Josep Bartolí, 1946

the sea. Tell me things, as much as you can. Your letters are in my eyes as if engraved with light, I adore them, they are my protection and my comfort and my life, until I can have you with me again, forever.

Is it already a fact that you'll leave on the 27th? Tell me that you're happy, tell me that you won't forget me, take care of yourself, my dear Bartolí, my heaven and my beloved child, I will miss your letters so much, and now they come from farther away, but don't stop writing for what you want most in the world, because I don't even want to think that things are going badly or that you're going to get sick, and I don't know anything. Don't keep me without news, I beg you with all my blood! I love you Bartolí, I love you, I love you. Call me soon so that my eyes look at you and my doves touch you – until the end.

I adore you
Mara

[In the left margin:] Bartolí my heaven, my beloved!

[In the right margin:] Hey my child, I have to scold you a little: my name is written like this: Frida Kahlo not Kalho. Don't forget it, my love.

JOSEP BARTOLÍ

Frida holding her dog

LETTER TO:

Carlos Pellicer

A Deep Affection

I sky you, so my wings extend enormously to love you without measure.

Carlos Pellicer, 1937

The poet Carlos Pellicer (1897–1977) shared a deep friendship with Frida, and they held great affection and admiration for one another. They remained close and he continued to visit her faithfully as her health declined toward the end of her life.

Carlos had known Diego since the 1920s; they were both founding members of the Grupo Solidario del Movimiento Obrero (Labour Movement Solidarity Group) in 1922, and Diego painted his portrait in 1936 and 1942. Born in Villahermosa, Tabasco, Carlos was deeply influenced by the Mexican Revolution and his country's rich history and landscapes. Besides being one of Mexico's most prominent poets, he was also an essayist, politician and promoter of the arts. He founded and designed several museums, served in various cultural institutions and, in his later years, was elected a senator.

Carlos and Frida became very close in the late 1940s and remained so until her death in 1954. He dedicated three sonnets to her in 1953, which she liked to keep under her pillow and share with visiting friends.[19] A few of the lines read:

> *You will always be alive on the Earth,*
> *Always a riot full of auroras,*
> *The heroic flower of successive dawns.*

After Frida's death, Diego asked Carlos to curate the Frida Kahlo Museum, entrusting him with the task of converting Frida's home into a public space. He was also the original curator of Anahuacalli, the museum that Diego created to display his collection of pre-Hispanic art.

1947
November

November 1947

I don't know how I dare to write to you, but yesterday we said that it would do me good.

Forgive the poverty of my words, I know that you will feel that I speak to you with my truth, which has always been yours, and that is what counts.

Is it possible to invent verbs? I want to tell you one:
I sky you, so my wings extend enormously to love you without measure.

I feel that from our place of origin we have been together, that we are made of the same matter, of the same waves, that we carry the same meaning within us. Your entire being, your prodigious genius and your humility are incomparable and enrich life; within your extraordinary world, what I offer you is just one more truth that you receive and that will always caress the deepest part of you. Thank you for receiving it, thank you for being alive, because yesterday you let me touch your most intimate light, and because you said with your voice and your eyes what I had been waiting for all my life.

To write to you, my name will be Mara. Ok?

If you ever need to give me your words, which would be for me the greatest reason to continue living, write to me without fear at… 'Poste restante', Coyoacán. Alright?

Wonderful Carlos,
Mara

Frida in bed, Coyoacán, 1952

Notes

1. Francisco Pimentel (1832–1893) was a Mexican writer and politician, and Alejandro lived on a street named after him. Writer and art historian Raquel Tibol suggests that 'Panchito Pimentel' was Frida's nickname for Alejandro's penis. (Kahlo and Tibol 2021, p. 35).

2. 'Se acabaron las pelonas' is a line from a popular refrain of the time. 'Pelona' means bald woman, and is what flappers were called in Mexico since they wore their hair short. 'La pelona' also refers to the personification of death.

3. A 'peladilla' is a sugared almond but is also a slang word meaning a vulgar woman.

4. 'La pelona', the bald woman, refers here to the personification of death.

5. A 'balero' is a traditional Mexican cup and ball toy.

6. Frida's sister Maty had run away with her boyfriend and was not in communication with the family for a while thereafter.

7. Grimberg 2008, p. 71.

8. Letter from Frida to Bert and Ella Wolfe dated 18 October 1934.

9. From 'Portrait of Diego', an essay written for the catalogue of the retrospective exhibition *Diego Rivera: 50 Years of Artistry*, held in the Palacio de Bellas Artes, August–December 1949. Also in Rivera 1960, p. 188.

10. Rivera 1960, p. 180.

11. Diego, as well as Frida and Cristina, were under suspicion after an attempt on Leon Trotsky's life. Diego fled to the USA with the assistance of the painter Irene Bohus and the actor Paulette Goddard.

12. Diego had a large collection of pre-Hispanic pieces that Frida packed up after he left for the USA.

13. 'Mam' is the nickname Nick gave to his photography lab manager, Marion Meredith, according to Grimberg 2002, p. 20.

14. Herrera 2002, p. 198.

15. Letter from Frida to Clifford Wight dated 11 April 1933.

16. Schneider and Noriega 1994.

17. Grimberg 2001, pp. 5–13.

18. Frida's letters to him were auctioned in 2015 by Doyle New York and sold to a private collector for US $137,000.

19. Grimberg 2008, p. 16.

Bibliography

Barbezat, Suzanne, *Frida Kahlo at Home*, Frances Lincoln, 2016

Deffebach, Nancy, *María Izquierdo and Frida Kahlo: Challenging Visions in Modern Mexican Art*, University of Texas Press, 2015

Grimberg, Salomon, *Frida Kahlo: Song of Herself*, Merrell, 2008

Grimberg, Salomon, *I Will Never Forget You: Frida Kahlo and Nickolas Muray*, Chronicle Books, 2002

Grimberg, Salomon, 'Jacqueline Lamba: From Darkness, with Light', *Woman's Art Journal*, vol. 22, no. 1, Spring–Summer 2001, pp. 5–13

Herrera, Hayden, *Frida: A Biography of Frida Kahlo*, Harper Perennial, 2002

Kahlo, Frida and Phyllis Freeman (ed.), *The Diary of Frida Kahlo: An Intimate Self-Portrait*, Harry N. Abrams, 1995

Kahlo, Frida, and Raquel Tibol, *Escrituras*, Cátedra Universitaria, 2021

Marnham, Patrick, *Dreaming with His Eyes Open: A Life of Diego Rivera*, University of California Press, 2000

Rivera, Diego with Gladys March, *My Art, My Life: An Autobiography*, Citadel Press, 1960

Robinson, Roxana, *Georgia O'Keeffe: A Life*, Brandeis University Press, 2020

Schneider, Luis Mario and Ricardo Noriega, *Frida Kahlo, Ignacio Aguirre: Cartas de una Pasión*, Trabuco y Clavel, 1994

Stahr, Celia, *Frida in America: The Creative Awakening of a Great Artist*, St. Martin's Press, 2020

Udall, Sharyn Rohlfsen, *Carr, O'Keeffe, Kahlo: Places of Their Own*, Yale University Press, 2001

Zamora, Martha, *The Letters of Frida Kahlo: Cartas Apasionadas*, Chronicle Books, 1995

Acknowledgements

I would like to express my sincere gratitude to everyone who contributed to making this book a reality. I have been extremely fortunate to have had the opportunity to work alongside a group of dedicated and talented individuals.

My heartfelt thanks go to Philip Cooper, publisher at Frances Lincoln, whose commitment and belief in this project kept the vision alive from the very beginning. Catherine Hooper, our managing editor, has been a joy to work with. Her keen editorial insight and thoughtful feedback have been invaluable. I'm equally grateful to Michael Brunstrom, senior editor at Quarto, whose patience and steady guidance shepherded this work to completion. Special thanks to Louise Evans, whose design expertise infused these pages with life and beauty, and to Sarah Bell for her tireless work sourcing photos and permissions.

I am truly grateful to Michelle Otero for her friendship and constructive feedback on parts of the manuscript, and to my sister, Sonya Barbezat, for her constant moral support and encouragement. Lastly, thank you to Benito, Jasmine and Jeronimo, for their patience, love and understanding throughout this journey. This book would not have been possible without their steadfast support.

Picture Credits

pp. 2, 87, 88, 91, 95, 99, 100, 107, 108, 111, 112, 115: Smithsonian: Archives of American Art, Nickolas Muray Papers

pp. 6, 77: akg-images

pp. 12, 152: Archivo Manuel Álvarez Bravo

pp. 15, 18, 21, 25, 26, 30, 33, 39 top, 43, 50, 53: Museo Dolores Olmedo/Banco de México, Fiduciario en el Fideicomiso relativo a los Museos Diego Rivera y Frida Kahlo

pp. 29, 66 bottom, 78, 148: Album/Alamy Stock Photo

p. 39 bottom: Reinhold Thiele/Stringer

pp. 40, 84: akg-images/fine-art-images

p. 47: Jorge Contreras Chacel/Bridgeman Images

p. 57: Graphic House/Getty Images

p. 58: Hulton Archive/Getty Images

p. 61: Bertram David Wolfe papers, 183, folder 6, dated 23 July 1935, Hoover Institution Library & Archives

p. 66 top: akg-images/Album

p. 69: Photo © Fine Art Images/Bridgeman Images

p. 74: Smithsonian: Archives of American Art, Emmy Lou Packard papers

p. 80: Photo Schalkwijk/Art Resource/Scala, Florence

p. 103: Lucas Vallecillos/Alamy Stock Photo

p. 118: Bettmann/Getty Images/© Georgia O'Keeffe Museum/DACS 2024

p. 120: Alfred Stieglitz/Georgia O'Keeffe Archive, Yale Collection of American Literature. Beinecke Rare Book and Manuscript Library

p. 124: Photo ©2024 Courtesy of The David and Alfred Smart Museum of Art, The University of Chicago / with the permission of the Bernard Silberstein Estate

p. 127: Album/Alamy Stock Photo

p.134: © succession Jacqueline Lamba, Courtesy Association Atelier André Breton/© ADAGP, Paris and DACS, London 2024

p. 136: akg-images/Erich Lessing

p. 140: akg-images

p. 142: Archivart/Alamy Stock Photo

p. 149: Bettmann/Getty images

p. 155: Photo Researchers/Getty Images

Quarto

First published in 2025 by Frances Lincoln,
an imprint of The Quarto Group.
One Triptych Place, London, SE1 9SH,
United Kingdom
T (0)20 7700 9000
www.Quarto.com

EEA Representation, WTS Tax d.o.o., Žanova ulica 3, 4000 Kranj, Slovenia

Text of introductory matter, notes, selection of letters by Frida Kahlo, translation (where applicable) copyright © 2025 Suzanne Barbezat
Illustrations copyright as listed on page 159
Design copyright © 2025 Quarto Publishing plc

Suzanne Barbezat has asserted her moral right to be identified as the Author of this Work in accordance with the Copyright Designs and Patents Act 1988.

All rights reserved. No part of this book may be reproduced or utilised in any form or by any means, electronic or mechanical, including photocopying, recording or by any information storage and retrieval system, without permission in writing from Frances Lincoln.

Every effort has been made to trace the copyright holders of material quoted in this book. If application is made in writing to the publisher, any omissions will be included in future editions.

A catalogue record for this book is available from the British Library.

ISBN 978-1-83600-154-6
Ebook ISBN 978-1-83600-155-3

10 9 8 7 6 5 4 3 2 1

P.2: Letter to Nickolas Muray, 31 May 1931

Design by Louise Evans

Publisher: Philip Cooper
Editor: Catherine Hooper
Senior Designer: Isabel Eeles
Production Controller: Alex Merrett

Printed in China